Implementing Labour Standards
in Construction

Implementing Labour Standards in Construction

A sourcebook

Sarah Ladbury, Andrew Cotton & Mary Jennings

Water, Engineering and Development Centre
Loughborough University
2003

Water, Engineering and Development Centre,
Loughborough University,
Leicestershire, LE11 3TU, UK

© WEDC, Loughborough University, 2003

Ladbury S., Cotton A.P. and Jennings M. (2003)
Implementing Labour Standards in Construction : A sourcebook
WEDC, Loughborough University, UK.

ISBN Paperback: 978 1 84380 017 0
ISBN Ebook: 978 1 78853 302 7
Book DOI: http://dx.doi.org/10.3362/9781788533027

A catalogue record for this book is available from the British Library.

A reference copy of this publication is also available online at:
http://www.lboro.ac.uk/wedc/publications/ilsic.htm

This document is an output from a project funded by the UK Department for International Development (DFID) for the benefit of low-income countries. The views expressed are not necessarily those of DFID. These documents are intended for general usage and readers are advised to use their own discretion when adopting any of the material contained herein and do so at their own risk.

WEDC (The Water, Engineering and Development Centre) at Loughborough University in the UK is one of the world's leading institutions concerned with education, training, research and consultancy for the planning, provision and management of physical infrastructure for development in low- and middleincome countries.

This edition is reprinted and distributed by Practical Action Publishing.
Since 1974, Practical Action Publishing has published and disseminated books and information in support of international development work throughout the world. Practical Action Publishing trades only in support of its parent charity objectives and any profits are covenanted back to Practical Action (Charity Reg. No. 247257, Group VAT Registration No. 880 9924 76).

About the authors

The SAC team

Sarah Ladbury (<u>sarahladbury@btinternet.com</u>) is a freelance social development consultant. She works on international development policy and operational issues in the public and private sector, mainly in South Asia, Sub-Saharan Africa, Europe and Central Asia. Employment practices and the implementation of labour standards, particularly within the construction sector, are areas of special interest and experience.

Andrew Cotton (<u>a.p.cotton@lboro.ac.uk</u>) is a Chartered Engineer with over twenty years experience in international development specialising in public health engineering and service provision for the urban poor, working mainly in the South Asia region. He works for WEDC (the Water, Engineering and Development Centre) at Loughborough University, where he is the Managing Director of the Department for International Development (DFID) Resource Centre in Water, Sanitation and Environmental Health.

Mary Jennings (<u>mjennings@eircom.net</u>) has extensive international experience in social development working as a practitioner, researcher, lecturer and trainer in Sub-Saharan Africa, East and South Asia, and Latin America. Much of her work has focused on institutional and poverty reduction issues, and the social benefits accruing from transport and infrastructure. She is currently a free lance consultant based in Dublin.

Acknowledgements

This sourcebook has been prepared by Sarah Ladbury, Mary Jennings and Andrew Cotton. Dr Sohail Khan of WEDC advised the authors throughout the preparation of the sourcebook, particularly on the development of contractual issues.

The Social Aspects of Construction study was funded jointly by the Infrastructure and Urban Development and the Social Development Departments of the UK Department for International Development. The research for this sourcebook has been conducted by a number of national country teams working within a common but broad framework and methodology. The SAC team would like to record their thanks to the following: the staff at the Department of Feeder Roads, Ghana especially Martin H Mensa; Steve Pollard of High Point Rendell; Ibrahim Akalbila of ISODEC. From India, our thanks go to Mr S.M. Vijayanand, IAS Member Secretary of the State Planning Board of Kerala and to the staff of the Socio-Economic Unit Foundation of Trivandrum, Kerala, especially Ms Suma Matthews and Ms Vijaya Venkataraman. From Zambia, the staff of CARE Zambia, especially Maric Kangamba. Our thanks also to the many people who participated at a workshop in Capetown in February 2002 at which the draft findings were presented. Also to those who contributed to the review of the draft document, in particular our colleagues at the ILO, from the EIIP in Geneva; ASIST Zimbabwe and Bangkok; to Robert Geddes (Scott Wilson), Peter Smith (DFID London) and Clare Barrington (DFID Mozambique). Sincere thanks also to Sue Cotton for her extensive editorial work on the final drafts of the sourcebook. Finally, a very special thanks to John Hodges (Chief Engineering Adviser), and Maria Cushion of DFID for supporting and overseeing the study.

Contents

Part 1. Introduction: Labour standards in construction

Defining the problem: the need to focus on labour standards   1

About this document   3

Who should read this document   5

More about labour standards   5

The meaning of each standard in practice   6

Part 2. Suggested action on implementing and monitoring labour standards

About Part 2 of the Sourcebook   11

Different forms of Contracting   11

Using the Sourcebook   13

Identifying gaps:

Action points 1 to 5   *16*

Defining the way ahead:

Action points 6 to 10   *25*

Implementing labour standards:

Action points 11 to 16   *36*

Monitoring labour standards:

Action points 17 to 19   *54*

Institutionalising labour standards:

Action point 20   *58*

Part 3. Contract clauses for labour standards

Using Part 3 of the Sourcebook   61

Section 1: Contract Clauses   63

Section 2: Making clauses operational   86

Section 3: HIV AIDS   89

Appendix 1

Sample Terms of Reference for a baseline study to address labour standards
in community contracting construction work   97

Appendix 2

Examples of Specification Clauses used in Bridges for
Feeder Roads project, Ghana   105

Part 1

Introduction

Labour standards in construction

Defining the problem: the need to focus on labour standards

Globally, the construction sector is one of the largest employers of temporary workers after agriculture. The majority of these workers in Africa, South Asia and Latin America work on a temporary basis: they are not registered as employees and have no formal employment protection. Without such protection millions work for wages which are not sufficient to meet basic needs, in dangerous conditions with no redress if they are injured or sick. Their temporary nature means that they may have no bargaining power and are generally not represented by trade unions; they cannot negotiate their wages, working hours or any other form of benefit. Women are particularly affected. The work they are allowed to do is often circumscribed by 'custom' and they are often paid at a lower rate than men. The construction sector is critically important to poor people as a provider of temporary employment; through the adoption of labour standards and being a good exemplar of 'decent work', it could play a key role in improving the livelihoods of poor people.

All those who work have a right to decent work. The concept of 'decent work', as used by the ILO, applies to all workers, including those on daily wages and in very temporary employment. It is work that is carried out in a safe physical environment with conditions which respect the rights of workers as defined in national law and international conventions.

The issue of labour standards raises legal, technical, economic, social and project management/supervision issues for construction work. For instance, it is connected to the legal agreements concerning procurement and conditions of contract. Technically, it is an issue of the adoption of the most appropriate technology in a particular situation given time, cost, and local development conditions. Economically and socially, by creating extensive employment, the construction sector has a major contribution to make towards poverty reduction and in the provision of social protection. In terms of management/supervision at the project level, task teams are ultimately responsible for making decisions concerning the design and supervision of projects including positive working conditions.

There is a high level of competition in the construction industry worldwide. In order to win bids contractors must keep their costs low and labour is often a major component of these costs. If, as is common, the client regularly awards contracts to the lowest bidder, contractors do their best to underbid their competitors. The winning tender may therefore be the one which pays the lowest wages, does not provide safety equipment or have coverage for accidents, and has the largest proportion of temporary workers – for whom no tax or social security is paid. Workers may be actively discouraged from joining unions or other associations that would give them a platform to negotiate for better conditions. In community contracting or self-help schemes using unpaid labour, there is frequently a lack of awareness of the necessity to apply national labour laws; minimal efforts are then made to protect the rights of workers.

The underlying problem is not a lack of labour law, which exists at international and national level. Rather, it is the lack of effective mechanisms to ensure that labour laws are applied and monitored. Ministries of Labour and Trade Unions typically have insufficient resources to inspect sites or represent workers outside the major towns, let alone address labour issues in community contracting or unpaid labour schemes. In this situation, the construction contract becomes a potentially important mechanism both for taking forward the implementation of labour standards and for demonstrating the benefits – for workers, contractors and the employer. Contract clauses that relate specifically to labour standards can be included and/or strengthened. Whilst this places formal responsibility on the contractor, it is important to develop a process around the contract which involves awareness raising for contractors, employers, community groups and workers, and which puts in place agreed mechanisms for monitoring compliance.

This document provides guidance on the collaborative process and contractual issues involved in implementing labour standards. Three different contexts for construction are considered:

- formal or conventional contracting;

- community contracting; and

- self-help schemes using unpaid labour.

Experience shows that even though labour standards are normally used in contexts where there is a clear employment relationship, they can also be applied in community contracting and self-help labour schemes. The ILO definition of community contracting is adopted in this document. Thus, community contracting is "… an agreement between a community and a contracting authority, whereby the community (or a section of the community) is responsible for the implementation of the works and therefore functions as a contractor". [1]

Whatever the context, implementing labour standards requires a collaborative effort between employers, supervisors, implementers, regulators and workers. The steps suggested in this document indicate practical and cost-effective procedures for bringing the relevant stakeholders together to implement and monitor labour standards. The aim is to contribute to the overall goal of providing 'decent work' for all workers in the construction industry.

About this document

The labour standards are based on international conventions of the International Labour Organisation (ILO). The majority are also covered in the national law of most countries.

The standards were first selected by DFID's Infrastructure and Urban Development Department in 1998 and their implementation has been piloted in three country programmes since that date: Ghana, Zambia and Kerala (India). The action suggested in relation to formal or conventional contracting is drawn largely from the pilot study in Ghana where the standards have been applied to a rural bridges programme and a larger feeder roads programme, both using standard contracting procedures. The action given in relation to community contracts is drawn largely from experience in Kerala where a massive programme of decentralisation has devolved responsibility for forty percent of infrastructure programmes to community level representatives and bodies. The action given in relation to self-help labour contracting draws on experience from Zambia where community contracting and standard contracting both operate within the urban water and sanitation sector. In addition to these pilot studies the action suggested draws on the experience of our many collaborators, particularly including our ILO partners, who have sought to improve the working conditions of construction workers in many different countries and types of programme.

---

[1] Source: Tournee, J and van Esch, W. "Community Contracts in Urban Infrastructure Works: Practical Lessons from Experience." ILO, 2000

Despite the generous time inputs of many people to this document, and the wide range of experience it draws upon, it remains 'work in progress'. Every time a decision is made to implement labour standards in an infrastructure programme something more is learned about how best to do this. This document should therefore be seen as part of an on-going process, a sincere but small effort to contribute to the provision of decent work and labour rights for some of the world's most vulnerable people.

The action points assume that a funding agency (e.g. a bilateral or multilateral development agency or a government), together with the employer/promoter (e.g. a line department of government, or utility) or, in the case of community contracting, a community, have identified labour standards in construction as a priority. The intention is to use the mechanism of the construction contract (whether formal, community-based or in self-help schemes) as a mechanism for the implementation and monitoring of labour standards.

The action points given in relation to contract clauses is based primarily on the Federation of Consulting Engineers (Federation Internationale des Ingenieurs Conseils, or FIDIC) Conditions of Contract for Works of Civil Engineering Construction (4th Edition 1987, reprinted 1992 with amendments). FIDIC 4th Edition, is widely used for international contracts and also forms the basis from which other sets of standard conditions are derived. World Bank standard bidding documents for the procurement of works for civil engineering construction ("SBDW"), (May 2000) are closely linked to FIDIC. Section 4 of SBWD reproduces the "Part 1 General Conditions" of the FIDIC 4th Edition. Section 5 of SBWD incorporates "Part 2 Conditions of Particular Application". In order to give a national (as opposed to purely international) dimension we have also included relevant material from construction contracts used in India and Ghana.

The action points suggested in this sourcebook provide generic advice for implementation and will need to be adapted for use on a case by case basis. This is allowed for through the suggested use of stakeholder consultation. In adapting the action points to a particular context it will be necessary to take account of differences in the regulatory framework, existing labour practice, the stakeholders involved, and the nature of the physical works.

Part 1 of the sourcebook provides the introduction and context to the development and use of labour standards with reference to construction.

Part 2 comprises a framework and detailed Action Points. This is the 'what to do' and 'how to do it' section, covering the process it is necessary to go through to implement labour standards in construction programmes.

Part 3 presents an analysis of contract clauses that have been used in relation to labour standards and suggests appropriate clauses to support the implementation of different labour standards. It includes guidance on developing specifications.

Who should read this document

This sourcebook has been written for those wanting to implement labour standards in programmes they fund, manage, supervise or implement. This includes:

- government officials involved in infrastructure procurement;

- procurement officers in International Financial Institutions and development agencies;

- other officials of development agencies involved with infrastructure, social protection or labour rights;

- representatives from employers' and workers' organisations;

- engineers and contract supervisors; and

- other technical and non-technical staff involved in the procurement and construction process.

More about labour standards

The action points in this sourcebook cover nine labour standards. The first four of these are stated in the Declaration on Fundamental Principles and Rights at Work, adopted by the ILO in 1998. Unlike an international labour convention that binds only members that ratify it, the Declaration applies automatically to all countries that have accepted the ILO Constitution. This means that all Member governments have pledged to respect, promote and realise these four standards. They are:

1. Freedom of Association and the effective recognition of the right to collective bargaining.

2. The elimination of all forms of forced or compulsory labour.

3. The effective abolition of child labour.

4. The elimination of discrimination in respect of employment and occupation.

In addition to these four standards, the action points cover five standards based on other international conventions of the ILO and on provisions contained in regional and national law. They are:

5. Health and safety to be addressed.

6. Wages to be paid in full and on time, to meet legal minima and be sufficient for basic needs.

7. Working hours to be limited; overtime to be paid.

8. No repeated casualisation to avoid meeting wages and other legal benefits.

9. All relevant social security regimes to be applied.

In addition to the above standards the action points also include a discussion of how to address HIV/AIDS in the construction industry.[2]

The meaning of each standard in practice

Some additional explanation is necessary to clarify what each standard means in practice. Each standard requires a point of reference to use as a benchmark. The basis of the labour standards covered in this sourcebook are the international conventions of the ILO. These serve as international benchmarks for states; governments signing up to these conventions undertake to reflect their provisions in national law.

Where governments do this - and national law exists on the issue - then this should be used as the primary reference point for a standard. If national law is not specific enough however, or if it is out of date, then a standard specified by the industry itself should be used. In this case the Collective Agreement between Employers' Associations for the industry and the relevant Trade Unions is the best benchmark. If neither national law nor a Collective Agreement can be used as a benchmark then the ILO Conventions should be used. But in this case some interpretation will be required as ILO conventions are not written to be applied to individual programmes in specific countries; they are written to be applicable internationally, and to be implemented by states.

An elaboration on what each standard means in practice is given in Box 1. The examples given have been taken from the Ghana pilot programme.

---

[2] Addressing HIV/AIDS is not a labour standard as such unless of course a person's HIV status is used to discriminate against them in which case the standard on discrimination applies. However, HIV/AIDS is included in this document because it is an important social issue in the sector. Construction workers are a high risk group for HIV due to the long periods of time many spend away from home. Ways of reducing the risk of HIV/AIDS to construction workers and communities can be addressed through the same consultation mechanisms as labour standards. This is the approach taken in this sourcebook.

Box 1. The 9 labour standards and HIV: what they mean in a construction context	
Labour standard[3]	**Practical implications (and reference to the main ILO conventions)**
1. Freedom of Association and the effective recognition of the right to collective bargaining.	This means that workers be allowed to establish and join work-based organisations if they wish. They can then use these to negotiate for wages and other working conditions. In practice this means that contractors should have a co-operative attitude to the construction workers' trade union, allow them onto sites to talk to workers, and allow workers to join unions or other work-based organisations. Note that this standard does not mean that workers have to join unions, just that they should have the right and opportunity to do so. (C87-Freedom of Association and Protection of the Right to Organise 1948; C98- Right to Organise and Collective Bargaining 1949; also relevant C135 - Worker's Repre-sentatives Convention 1971). In some contexts, workers may opt to be represented by a local collective or community group and these should be recognised as legitimate negotiating bodies[4].
2. The elimination of all forms of forced or compulsory labour.[5]	The ILO definition of forced labour is any work that is extracted under the menace of penalty – or where the people have not offered themselves voluntarily. In practice this can happen when a contractor forces workers to do overtime or a 7 day week without their consent and under threat of penalty, e.g. job loss. (C29-Forced Labour Convention 1930; C105 - Abolition of Forced labour Convention 1957).
3. The effective abolition of child labour.	The ILO definition of a child is a person of 14 years or under. If hazardous work is involved then the minimum age is 18 years. In practice child labour can occur if women bring their children to site and they 'help' with a particular activity, e.g. breaking stones. But if stopping this practice prevents women from working then dialogue is vital: it may be that alternative action needs to be taken in order to ensure women themselves do not lose their jobs, e.g. through making alternative child care arrangements available. (C138 - Minimum Age 1973; C182 - Worst Forms of Child Labour 1999).

[3] For more information on the ILO Declaration and international labour standards contact the ILO International Labour Standards Department, Email: normes@ilo.org Website:www.ilo.org - then click on 'Standards and Fundamental Principles'.

[4] In many rural areas, there is no trade union representation but workers may form a collective to enhance their bargaining power, and it is important that these local negotiating bodies are recognised.

[5] There is a connection between forced labour and payment in full and on time (points 2 and 6 of box 1). Failure to pay on time is common and is well documented in some countries (e.g. India, Nepal). It results in workers having to borrow from the labour agents or contractors who employ them. Indebtedness in turn creates obligations and the workers can become, in effect 'bonded' to their employer; a situation which can lead to forced labour.

Box 1. continued	
Labour standard	**Practical implications (and reference to the main ILO conventions)**
4. The elimination of discrimination in respect of employment and occupation.	Discrimination means denying someone a job or training on the basis of a factor which does not affect their ability to do that job. For example, because they are from a particular region or ethnic group, or because they are a woman. In practice discrimination is often justified in terms of culture, e.g. 'our women like to carry concrete' implying they will not be considered for other jobs. Such an attitude is discriminatory if it results in limiting employment opportunities for a particular group. (C 100 - Equal Remuneration 1951; C111 - Discrimination (Employment and Occupation 1958).
5. Health and safety to be addressed.	Workplaces must be safe and without risk of injury to employees. National labour law will normally state minimum requirements for protective clothing and safety precautions specific to the industry. In Ghana for example, basic protective clothing for construction includes steel toe-capped boots, overalls, gloves and raincoats for wet weather work. Additional clothing is required for specific tasks. The contractor must also train one employee as safety officer and one to be responsible for first aid (with a properly equipped first aid box). The provision of potable water, latrines on site and emergency procedures in the event of accident are also prescribed in law. Where the law does not provide an adequate standard then the Collective Agreement between the Employers' Association and the trade union is the best point of reference. (C155 - Occupational Health and Safety 1981; C167 - Safety and Health in Construction 1988. There is also an 'ILO Code of Practice on Safety and Health in Construction 1992' which covers safety and health planning, co-ordination and compliance.)
6. Wages to be paid in full and on time, to meet legal minima and be sufficient for basic needs.	Where there is a current national minimum wage then this can be used as a standard. However, high inflation may mean that the rate is out of date. In this case the rate agreed in the relevant Collective Agreement should be applied. If there is no such agreement then the rate used by a local construction company known for good practice may be an alternative reference point. Wages should be paid in cash, not in kind. (C131 - Minimum Wage Fixing Convention ; C95 - Protection of Wages Convention 1949); C94 - Labour Clauses - Public Contracts. Note that C94, ratified by Ghana, also requires that notices be displayed on site to inform workers about their contract conditions.)

Box 1. continued	
Labour standard	**Practical implications (and reference to the main ILO conventions)**
7. Working hours to be limited; overtime to be paid.	National law will specify the 'working week' - usually 40 - 42 hours. Overtime should be paid above this rate according to the national legal formula. Regulations should ensure that the use of task-based/piecework does not lead to self-exploitation and workers having to spend longer hours than specified in the legislation. (C14 - Weekly Rest (Industry) 1921, C1 - Hours of Work (Industry) 1919, also C47).
8. No repeated casualisation to avoid meeting wages and other legal benefits.[6]	This standard is to tackle a common practice - in Ghana as elsewhere - whereby workers are engaged for months or years on a series of temporary contracts so their employer can avoid paying tax or social security. It means the worker - called a casual but more accurately a 'temporary worker', is typically paid less than permanent workers, and ends up with no pension rights or access to other benefits e.g. accident insurance. (C102 - Social Security (Minimum Standard) 1952; C957 - Maintenance of Social Security - Rights 1982.)
9. All relevant social security regimes to be applied.	All countries have laws regarding registration for social security and these should be followed. In Ghana there is a problem as the law does not allow for temporary workers, it states that all workers must be registered for social security no matter how short their period of paid employment. This was very difficult to apply on the Bridges project, not least because those employed for very short periods could not see the point of registering given the 20 year rule to qualify for a pension. As a result of this DFID is funding a study to review, with regulators, how to make regulations on social protection relevant and feasible for all workers. (ILO conventions as above.)

---

[6] It is acknowledged that informal (verbal), short term contracts, without benefits, are the norm in the construction industry in many countries. However, standard number 8 seeks to make a distinction between the true casual worker (hired on a daily basis for a short period) and a temporary worker (hired more or less continually by the same employer for months or years) who is treated as a casual, i.e. with none of the benefits of formal employment. The action points seek to encourage employers to 'move' this group of temporary workers into the permanent worker category.

Box 1. continued	
Labour standard	**Practical implications (and reference to the main ILO conventions)**
10. HIV/AIDS to be addressed.	The ILO's 'Code of Practice' on AIDS recognises HIV/AIDS as a workplace issue and goes beyond awareness raising to include non-discrimination, confidentiality, care and support.[7] UNAIDS and other agencies produce guidelines of employer good practice with regard to HIV/AIDS. The ideal is to follow the national policy on AIDS if this has been developed. In Ghana, as per national policy, the Ministry of Roads and Transport will apply for funding from the Ghana AIDS Commission to mount an education campaign for contractors, workers and communities. In the meantime, and as a stop-gap activity, contractors must allow health staff to visit sites and inform workers about the risks of HIV/AIDS. Workers are to be paid for time spent on HIV/AIDS awareness.

[7] To access the ILO 'Code of Practice' on HIV/AIDS go to www.ilo.org, click on *Technical Programmes*, then *Social Protection*, then *HIV/AIDS and the World of Work*. The full code can be read in English, French or Spanish.

Suggested action on implementing and monitoring labour standards

About Part 2 of the Sourcebook

This part of the Sourcebook, which offers guidance on implementing labour standards, is structured as follows:

- Different forms of contracting. Definitions and descriptions of the three different contracting situations are presented, namely: formal or conventional contracting; community contracting; and self-help labour schemes.

- Using the Sourcebook. In this section, Box 2 summarises the key issues, what to do about them, and how to do it. The 'how to do it' columns make reference to specific numbered action points which are grouped according to the three different situations listed above.

- Action Points. Detailed 'how to do it' action points are then listed separately.

Different forms of contracting

This Sourcebook is based on the experience of reviewing and implementation of labour standards in three different contexts:

- formal or conventional contracting;

- community-based contracting; and

- self-help, unpaid labour schemes.

Formal or conventional contracting. The most commonly used procedures for the procurement of infrastructure are those which lead to the award of contracts through competitive tender. Most engineering contracts recognize a 'triangle of actors':

- *Employer (or Promoter);*

- *Engineer;* and

- *Contractor.*

A typical case involves a government department letting a contract to a private sector contractor for the construction of infrastructure. Government is the *employer/promoter*; they have planned and designed the work, and are paying for it to be implemented. Government appoints an *Engineer* to represent their interests; this person is usually in the full time employment of the relevant government department, although private sector consultants may fulfill this role on behalf of the promoter in larger engineering works. In accordance with the government (or financing agency) procedures laid down, a *contractor* is appointed through a competitive bidding process to do the actual construction work. The contractor will normally be listed on a register of contractors who are regarded as sufficiently competent to carry out the work envisaged.

Community-based contracting in the context of this sourcebook is when the role which the contractor fulfils in the formal or conventional approach is taken on by a group of individuals who come together for the purpose of constructing the infrastructure. We are therefore using the ILO definition of a Community Contract as one where "…there is an agreement between a community and a contracting authority, whereby the community (or a section of the community) is responsible for the implementation of the works and therefore functions as a contractor".[8] Community Contracting is one where the group members are paid for their labour. This normally only happens when the works to be constructed are: small (often referred to as *minor works*); involve only simple and primarily unskilled tasks; and are not of a hazardous nature. The group of people who come together are often from the same community – hence the term community contracting; they may also be employed by a community based organisation. Such groups are not registered as commercial entities and do not normally bid for work in the same way as a conventional commercial contractor.

---

[8] Source: Tournee, J and W. van Esch 'Community Contracts in Urban Infrastructure Works", ILO 2000

Self-help labour schemes in the context of this sourcebook refers to community-based contributions of unpaid labour. The contribution of unpaid work by community members underpins the approach adopted by many NGOs, and more recently by bilateral and multilateral programmes, to the development of community infrastructure. It is seen to be a way of promoting community ownership, with the rationale that local participation ensures that the project responds to a real community need, includes an element of cost sharing, and builds the community's capacity for maintenance.

Using the Sourcebook

The action points proposed are not a step by step methodology leading to guaranteed success; we are dealing with a set of processes, and local circumstances will dictate the precise details.

Box 2 identifies the five key steps which are involved in implementing labour standards.[9] These are:

- Identify gaps
- Define the way ahead
- Implement labour standards
- Monitor standards
- Institutionalise labour standards in the sector

For each of these key steps, Box 2 below guides you to what to do, and how to do it through reference to the set of Action Points which are presented in the following section.

---

[9] The action points are written as though the decision to implement labour standards is made right at the beginning of the contractual process. They also assume that all 9 labour standards will be implemented. In practice we know that a decision to implement labour standards can start half way through an infrastructure programme (perhaps in response to a labour issue that is covered in the contract but which has never been properly implemented and monitored before). Similarly, in practice, there may be an initial decision to focus on some standards and not others. Obviously readers will need to use this sourcebook in ways which meet their needs; not all these steps will be relevant in all circumstances.

Box 2. Finding your way about the Action Points section of this document

Issue	What to do	Where to find it		
		Formal contracting	Community contracting	Self-help schemes (unpaid)
A. Identifying gaps. Namely those practices that are detrimental to ensuring decent work for the construction workforce in the project location (i.e. detrimental practices currently occurring on sites where there is no specific attempt to apply labour standards). This will make clear which standards to focus on.	■ review national labour laws - and policy on HIV/AIDS. ■ review standard contract documents. ■ review relevant Collective Agreements between Trade Unions/other worker negotiating bodies, and Employers. ■ research typical site practice; what standards are applied at present? To which categories of worker?	AP 1 AP 2 AP 4 AP5	AP1 AP3 N/A AP5	AP1 AP3 N/A AP5
B. Defining the way ahead. This means identifying the stakeholders and agreeing their roles. It also means preparing to address the needs of different categories of worker, particularly those least protected, i.e. casuals and unpaid workers.	■ identify the stakeholders and their interests. ■ identify stakeholder roles and responsibilities (special reference to community contracting and self-help schemes). ■ identify which labour standards to focus on. ■ consider how temporary and unpaid workers can realise their rights.	AP 6 AP 7 AP 8 AP 10	AP 6 AP 7 AP9 AP 10	AP6 AP7 AP9 AP 10
C. Implementing labour. standards These six activities need to take place in parallel.	■ develop and budget for a consultation process. ■ anticipate the concerns of stakeholders. ■ build the capacity of stakeholders to implement labour standards. ■ incorporate labour standards in contract documents and community contracting agreements. ■ cost each labour standard and agree who will pay. ■ ensure communities and workers are informed about their rights.	AP 11 AP 12 AP 13 AP 14 AP 15 AP 16	AP 11 AP 12 AP 13 AP 14 AP 15 AP 16	AP 11 AP 12 AP 13 N/A AP 15 AP 16

Box 2. Continued

Issue	What to do	Where to find it		
		Formal contracting	Community contracting	Self-help schemes (unpaid)
D. Monitoring standards. Two forms of monitoring are required:	■ monitor for compliance. ■ consider introducing incentives and sanctions. ■ monitor the impact of standards on workers and communities.	AP17 AP18 AP19	AP17 AP18 AP19	AP 17 N/A AP19
E. Institutionalising labour standards.	■ scaling up.	AP20	AP20	Not recommended

The Action Points

A. Identifying gaps

The following steps are suggested to identify existing 'gaps'. Broadly, these comprise issues around:

- the legislative and policy framework;

- contractual processes;

- existence of relevant agreements; and

- current site practice.

Action Points 1-5 are included in this 'identifying gaps' section.

Action Point 1. Review national labour law and policy on HIV/AIDS

We recommend you contact either the ILO office if there is one in the country, the Ministry of Labour or the national Trade Union Congress (Information Department) for information about how to get copies of relevant labour laws and Collective Agreements. Contact the national HIV/AIDS office if there is one for national initiatives on HIV/AIDS. It is useful to have a copy of the ILO Code of Practice as a reference, particularly if a national policy has still to be developed.

Conventional and community contracting
Review national labour laws and policy on HIV/AIDS

√ Identify legal and regulatory issues concerned with each standard . This will include (but is not restricted to):
- labour laws in relation to construction workers, working hours, payment of wages, minimum wages, inter-state migration legislation (if relevant);

- social security such as workmen's compensation, welfare acts;

- health/accident insurance schemes and whether there is provision for informal sector/casual workers to participate;

- child labour legislation;

- equality legislation such as equity in remuneration, equal opportunities (gender, disability, migrants); and

- trade union/freedom of association legislation.

√ Identify both national and any sector commitments made regarding HIV/AIDS.

√ Identify areas which are not well covered or where the law is out of date (a typical example is the minimum wage; where there is high inflation this is unlikely to provide for 'basic needs' and an alternative point of reference will be necessary).

√ If there is no national AIDS policy then identify the most appropriate organisation with guidance on addressing HIV/AIDS in the construction sector (e.g. ILO, UNAIDs, SAfAIDS). [10]

As labour law rarely comes in a single legislative instrument, it is likely that the nine labour standards will be covered in several different pieces of legislation.

Community contracting

Labour legislation in many countries provides comprehensive protection to workers in the formal contracting sector, although implementation and monitoring are frequently lacking. When works are implemented at the community level, the legal and regulatory framework for protecting workers rights, and responsibility for enforcement or overseeing such rights, is usually less clear. But in many countries national law will offer different forms of protection to such workers - it is just a question of finding it. It may not be termed 'labour law' but may come under laws relating to welfare or social security. It is crucial to find all national legislation which relates to the rights of workers in all forms of contracting.

Self-help schemes using unpaid labour

National labour laws do not normally cover unpaid work. The application of labour standards in this context gives rise to two issues:

■ In agreeing to do unpaid work a person agrees to forego one labour standard – that of a fair/minimum wage. But this does not mean that they lose their entitlement to other rights.

---

[10] For best industry practice on HIV/AIDS, including current practice in specific countries contact unaids@un.org
Guidance and best practices on HIV/AIDS is also available on the ILO website (www.ilo.org).

- A key question is what is sensible and reasonable to expect of communities in terms of unpaid work. There is need to distinguish between short term unpaid work which is likely to be acceptable to communities if worked out in close consultation, and long term unpaid work which is likely to undermine livelihoods. See Box 3.

Box 3.   Unpaid labour in a water and sanitation programme, Lusaka

Unpaid labour contribution was part of the partnership agreement between the international donor and the local communities. However, the level of labour required by the project was such that households were obliged to work on a daily basis for several (6-9) months. The burden of this work fell to women who work in or near the settlements while men go outside in search of paid work. Communities eventually abandoned the approach on the basis that it prevented them from earning other sources of income and was unsustainable, and instead adopted a policy of paying labourers.

The following questions can provide guidance in deciding which kind of labour should be used:

- What is the scale and frequency of the works? If the work is a once-off effort by the community to support community infrastructure, unpaid work may be used e.g. painting a classroom, or cleaning drains. If the work is going to take place over a long-term or requires repeated work, it should be paid.

- How complex and safe are the tasks? If tasks are risky, they should be done by skilled paid workers and not by unskilled unpaid labourers who are contributing their work in the interests of the community.

- What standard of work is to be achieved? Can it be done by unpaid unskilled workers or does it need skilled workers?

- How will unpaid work affect the capacity of individuals and households to earn a living? If communities are over-burdened, their capacity to undertake other income earning activities will be affected, and ultimately they may be disempowered.

- What are the opportunity costs to communities of delayed access to benefits because work carried out on an unpaid basis takes longer to implement.

- Who is sponsoring the project and what are the power relations – is there really a choice for community members to contribute unpaid labour, or implicitly, is there a requirement of forced labour e.g. if the community does not contribute unpaid labour, will they be denied the infrastructure? Distinguish between locally initiated self-help groups and large scale projects sponsored by large international agencies.

- What is the objective of adopting an unpaid approach - is it to confirm that communities will value and maintain the infrastructure, or creating structures for long term development, or saving costs?[11]

- From a development perspective, should unpaid work be considered when economies are in a downturn and the informal sector is already over-burdened? Rather, shouldn't the project be contributing to livelihoods by creating jobs?

If the answer to these questions suggests that the community are being offered an unfair deal, rethink the approach to unpaid work and consider the concept of community contracting as an alternative.[12]

In summary, points to take into account when deciding on whether to use unwaged or paid labour are:

√ Define the boundaries of the work - should it really be unpaid?

√ Assess the intensity of the impact on livelihoods - don't force people into long-term commitments that affects their livelihoods.

√ Don't make unpaid work a scapegoat for good governance where local authorities are reneging on their responsibilities to provide services to its citizens.

---

[11] We recognise that there is another option which is halfway between unwaged and waged labour. This is when the workforce agree to a wage lower than the statutory minimum with the difference regarded as a 'community contribution' to a project. In this way it is possible to achieve the community ownership and cost-cutting objectives of unpaid labour but also provide some much-need cash for workers.

[12] An additional indicator related to the decision about the use of paid or unpaid labour concerns the future use of the constructed asset (a kind of guaranteed user right). For example, a community constructs a water kiosk using unpaid labour but after construction the government transfers all drinking water assets to a water company who can establish and adjust the water price. In this case the community would have increased the assets of the private company through their unpaid labour with the company then having the right to set prices. This would not, of course, have been the intention, at least in the eyes of the community. In such circumstances there needs to be a guarantee that the community is able to use the asset they have created according to pre-determined and agreed conditions.

Action Point 2. Review standard contract documents (formal contracting)

√ Identify the key contract documents in use for procurement of works and the circumstances in which they are used. Examples include: standard conditions of contract used by line departments, utilities and local government; international contracts such as FIDIC; donor–specific contracts such as the World Bank standard bidding documents for the procurement of civil works ("SBDW").

√ Identify existing references to labour standards in the contracts used for the type of physical works proposed. General Conditions of Contract will usually give an overview of what coverage there is, but it is the Special Conditions (or Conditions of Particular Application) where any details will be specified in relation to local circumstances.

√ Establish the priority of contract documents; for example in FIDIC and SBDW, Part 2 Conditions of Particular Application take precedence over the provisions of Part 1 General Conditions (see also action point 14).

√ Identify whether any of the standard specifications which accompany the commonly used forms of contract make any more detailed reference to the adoption of labour standards, for example in relation to the provision of water, sanitation, health and safety equipment etc.

√ If labour standards are mentioned, see whether the documentation specifies how the various items are to be priced. For example, are they part of the contractors overhead? Are they included as Bill of Quantities items and hence as part of the bidding process? Are they prime cost items? Is it obligatory on the employer to provide the necessary items outside of the contract?

√ A crucial issue is to determine whether the contract clauses are not making adequate provision for labour standards, or whether the standards are there but are not monitored or enforced.

√ Therefore, enquire about examples of monitoring and enforcement; if this occurs, find out who carried out the monitoring. This is important in order to establish the extent of national and local monitoring capacity.

We have reviewed a number of standard conditions of contract to try to illustrate the range of clauses which exist in relation to labour standards. These include:

- Federation of Consulting Engineers (Federation Internationale des Ingenieurs Conseils, or FIDIC) Conditions of Contract for Works of Civil Engineering Construction (4th Edition 1987, reprinted 1992 with amendments). FIDIC 4th Edition, is widely used for international contracts and also forms the basis from which other sets of standard conditions are derived.

- World Bank standard bidding documents for the procurement of works for civil engineering construction ("SBDW"), (May 2000). Section 4 of SBWD reproduces the "Part 1 General Conditions" of the FIDIC 4th Edition. Section 5 of SBWD incorporates "Part 2 Conditions of Particular Application" along with amendments introduced by the World Bank.

- Those used by the Government of Ghana in their Feeder Roads Bridges project which is funded by a bilateral donor (the Department for International Development of the UK government).

- Those used by the Public Works Departments in the Indian states of Orissa and Kerala.

This review is contained in Part 3 of this document. Even if you are not using any of the conditions of contract mentioned above, we recommend that you look at this material as it will guide you through a review of other conditions of contract.

Action Point 3. Review contract documents (community contracting)

In contrast to the formal contracting sector which has a legislative, procedural and contractual framework that can be used to introduce labour standards, the vehicles for promotion of such standards in community contracting are less clear. There may be no formalised approach such as competitive bidding. Some community contracts are based on written contracts mirroring (to some extent) the approach of the formal sector, while others are less formal arrangements and can include verbal agreements to carry out particular activities; these are also a form of contract. Hence:

√ It is essential to review the agreements and contracts which are in use for community-based work.

√ An important point to look for relates to the definition of the parties to the contract; in particular, the group that takes on the role of contractor. It is usually the case that a Community Based Organisation (CBO) or other concerned groups need to be registered as a legal entity under national/local law in order for that group to become a party to the contract. In the absence of this, whilst it may be clear that it is the intention of the CBO or local group to take on the role of contractor, any contract document which is signed by an individual implies that the individual is legally acting in his/her own capacity. In other words, it is this individual, not the CBO/group, which is taking on the liabilities of the contract. These individuals are usually unaware of the legal obligations and liabilities implied in contract, and in practice it is unreasonable to expect them to meet liabilities, as they are community members who are acting in the interests of the community. In such cases, it is essential to put the necessary measures in place to ensure that these people are not exposed, the most obvious of which are health and safety measures and accident insurance.

Introducing labour standards in unpaid work is problematic; in the absence of a contract with the community, the focus must be on promoting buy-in by community leaders.

√ Create awareness of the need to adopt labour standards with community leaders, those overseeing the works, and workers.

√ Encourage a sense of association such that community groups can negotiate arrangements for workers.

Action Point 4. Review relevant collective agreements between trade unions and employers

There may be more than one trade union representing workers in the construction sector. It is necessary to contact all trade unions and employers' associations relevant to the work on site. Contact details of trade unions can be obtained from the national Trade Union Congress. Information can also be obtained from the international trade secretariats (ITS). The relevant ITSs are: The International Federation of Building and Woodworkers (IFBWW) and the International Federation of Chemical, Energy, Mine and General Workers (IFCEM).[13] It is however important to recognise that other groups may exist that represent workers, especially in areas where trade unions do not exist, that will need to be consulted.

---

[13] International Trade Secretariats are amongst the oldest international trade union organisations. ITSs give support to the implementation of labour standards and see a strong trade union organisation as essential to ensuring that decent work is achieved and observed. Most have programmes of support for their affiliate unions in developing countries. They are a valuable source of information on labour standard issues in their sector. (Contact details: IFBWW in Geneva. Email: infor@ifbww.org. Website: http://www.ifbww.org IFCEM in Brussels. Email:icem@geo2.poptel.org.uk Website: http://www.icem.org)

√ Identify labour standards noted in the Collective Agreement/s.

√ Compare the agreement with national law and make a particular note of clauses in the Collective Agreements that are more up-to-date or detailed than in national law. Where there are gaps in legislation, the agreement can be used to identify the appropriate standard.

√ Engage all relevant Trade Unions/worker representatives and Employers' Associations in dialogue about the intended objectives of the programme. These groups are important to engage with in the early stages. Identify their interest in becoming part of the wider stakeholder group (see next section on implementation).

√ Ascertain what proportion of workers in the sector are unionised and where they are located. (This will indicate whether construction contractors are likely to have any familiarity with labour standards as a result of having unionised workers on site.)

Action Point 5. Research typical site practice

Whatever the law or collective agreements specify, practices on site tend to be different. Typical site practice for the sort of physical works (and categories of contractor) being considered must be understood. For example, do contractors regularly provide the most basic safety clothing? Is it worn? Do contractors keep records (employment, wage rates, accidents, deductions)? What are contractor attitudes to unions or other forms of organisation?

√ Contact the Employers Association for information of classes of contractors, the numbers contractors typically employ, their geographical distribution, and information on employment practices and labour conditions on sites. Information on classes of contractors might also be obtained from the requisite Ministry where contractors are registered and classed, for example, the Ministry of Works. The number of workers registered as employees (i.e. with social security certificates) is likely to be much lower than the number actually employed.

√ Conduct a rigorous search for any previous research on site conditions. If nothing is available because this type of exercise has never been conducted before, be prepared to conduct a baseline survey. See Box 4. This need not be an extensive or time consuming exercise and there is no need for a long questionnaire. A few questions systematically asked of a distributive sample of individuals on selected sites will identify the main issues. The legal and regulatory framework for each of the nine labour standards can then be compared with common practice on sites. Either local consultants or technical staff will be able to carry out this work provided they speak the local language/s. Interviews will need to be conducted with representatives of the client (government officials/NGOs/donor), implementers (contractors/community based groups), and workers (of all categories).

Box 4.   The Ghana Baseline Survey

In Ghana a short questionnaire was supplemented by informal interviews with site agents and workers on 40 rural sites. The survey was undertaken by Department of Feeder Roads Assistant Engineers and funded by DFID. It showed that:

■ repeated casualisation was commonplace - indeed, only a handful of workers were registered for tax and social security at each site; some workers had been with the same employer for many years but were still on daily wages;

■ rates of pay and other conditions varied significantly depending on the contractor; and

■ few contractors kept any form of records.

This gave an overview of the scale of issues to be addressed. It also showed that in most cases 8 of the 9 labour standards were not being addressed. The only exception was child labour - no-one under 15 was found working on these sites - and it was known that children were not employed on road construction elsewhere in Ghana.

√ If possible, ensure that the baseline survey is both designed and carried out by engineering and technical staff.

A baseline survey would typically be seen as an activity for a social scientist. However, giving responsibility for the survey to engineering and technical staff can help ensure they buy-in to the process from the start, and develop an understanding of labour issues. They will be able to use their practical construction experience to design the most appropriate survey for the circumstances. Their involvement in identifying labour standard gaps will also help them design effective solutions.

In many countries the engineering profession has limited exposure to formal education on labour standards, as technical training and professional development tends to focus on technical issues. It is also possible that contract procedure is not wholly understood, particularly by more junior site staff. It is critical for the success of implementation that the technical staff who will be supervising the contract understand the need to implement labour standards. As such, if the baseline survey is carried out by a member of the engineering profession it will tend to have more credibility with those staff who will ultimately have to implement contract conditions.

Draft terms of reference for commissioning such a study are included in Appendix 1 "Sample Terms of Reference for a baseline study to address labour standards in construction work".

B. Defining the way ahead

The following steps are suggested to assist in defining the way ahead. Broadly, these comprise issues around identifying:

- stakeholders - and their roles and responsibilities;

- which labour standards to focus on; and

- particular issues to consider regarding temporary and unpaid workers.

Action Points 6-10 are included in this "Defining the way ahead" section.

Action Point 6. Identify stakeholders and their interests

There is a need to identify the stakeholders, both primary and secondary, and determine their interests. Note that stakeholders in community contracting and self-help schemes may not be as easily identified as in the formal contracting sector, where the labourers on the contractor's payroll are identifiable as the primary stakeholders.

At the project level, there are usually three broad groups of stakeholders:

- the labourers (skilled/unskilled, male/female);

- the client (e.g. local government or line departments, NGO, donor); and

- contractor/sub-contractors (the implementing group).

We have not separated out 'the community' as a separate stakeholder because, depending on the type of contracting, community members will typically be involved in one or more of the roles above. For example, in both formal and community contracting, community members will normally provide labour and may even be sub-contractors (formal contracting) or implementers (as a CBO in community contracting). In self-help schemes different community members may take on, in effect, all three roles.

At national, state or provincial level, government bodies have responsibilities in relation to construction work. Such stakeholders need to be identified and informed of the interest in promoting labour standards, and their support elicited; most especially they need to be informed of the findings of the baseline study.

Government bodies will include all those linked with the project and/or promoting poverty reduction such as the Local Authority, the Public Works Department, procurement advisers, Water/Electricity/Roads Departments, and the Labour Department. National professional Associations are another important group of stakeholders (of Employers, Contractors, and Workers). Also at a national level insurance companies and social security agents will have an interest as they provide social protection, and it will be necessary to assess how their services can support compliance with labour standards.

At the local level, contractors (who may be large equipment based, or small scale/ petty contractors), engineers and site managers, have important interests as they are responsible for implementing the contract, and their capacity and concerns must be considered.

At an advocacy level, stakeholders may include trade unions, community associations, workers representatives, the research community, media, NGOs, and other donors. It is important to recognise organisations that have social acceptability to represent workers; these may be other than trade unions which are not necessarily found in all contexts e.g. in community contracting.

√ Undertake a stakeholder analysis at the outset to determine:
  - stakeholders at the project level; and
  - wider stakeholders that may influence the adoption of labour standards.

√ Make a note of the interests of the different stakeholders. Identify those which can be relied upon to support the labour standards initiative. Are any likely to oppose it? Think through the reasons for their opposition and based on this develop a strategy to incorporate them as the initiative gets underway.

√ Make a note of the different roles that each stakeholder can play.

Action Point 7. Identify stakeholder roles and responsibilities (with special reference to community contracting and self-help schemes)

In formal contracting the contract will set out the roles and responsibilities of the various parties very clearly. The review of standard contract documents under-taken through action point 2 will identify these. For example, contractors are legally liable for labour standards and usually take measures to protect their companies, while the Labour Department is legally responsible for enforcement (though rarely has the capacity to do this). However, with community contracting and self-help schemes roles and responsibilities are less clear.

In community contracting, the key issue is the implication of transferring liability from an organised and regulated construction sector to an inexperienced commu-nity structure. Such liability is rarely considered, but as mentioned earlier, contractually and thus legally, liability lies with community representatives who undertake the contract on behalf of the community. Such groups or individuals are voluntary, and work in the interests of the community. However, they tend to have an informal structure and may not be a legal entity, are usually unaware of this legal liability, and have neither the indemnity nor the resources in the event of a claim. Thus, both they and the workers can become victims if labour standards are violated e.g. if there is a serious accident with no insurance coverage. In other words, assumed and actual liability is often very different in these circumstances.

Because people involved in community contracting tend to know each other, social relationships function as one of the strongest mechanisms to safeguard at least some of the rights of workers. On the other hand, pressure can be exerted on individuals not to make claims against community leaders even when there is permanent disability e.g. in case of an accident, workers are often left to pay for medical treatment themselves as well as bear the cost of lost income.

Having identified the various stakeholders, both primary and secondary:

√ determine the parties to the contractual relationship and who is liable for what;

√ with each stakeholder clarify their roles and responsibilities with regard to labour standard implementation;

√ agree, and put in place measures that protect workers and community repre-sentatives. Ensure project costs include provision for death/accident/ medical insurance if existing social security arrangements will not provide for this.

Action Point 8. Identify which standards to focus on (formal contracting)

The on-site survey will indicate key labour standard issues that could be addressed through contractual mechanisms.

√ Compare the findings of the site survey with the standards contained in national law and the Collective Agreement/s. Identify the major gaps in labour standard implementation/provision - these will indicate the areas of focus.

√ Agree which standards to focus on with all the important stakeholders. Hold a workshop to do this. Everyone needs to begin the implementation process fully aware of what the current situation is and what the goals are. Box 5 describes the consultation process adopted in Ghana.

Box 5. The Ghana consultation process

In Ghana the first stakeholder workshop was held in 1998. The Employer, the Department of Feeder Roads (DFR), hosted the 2 day discussion on exactly what standards it was feasible to try and achieve on the DFID assisted Feeder Roads Bridges programme. This workshop brought together:

- DFR engineers (the Employer)

- the Association of Contractors

- the Construction and Building Material Worker's Union

- the Ministry of Labour

- the Department of Social Security

- DFID (the funder)

- the EC (who were funding adjacent works under a Stabex programme, also implemented by DFR).

- an NGO (ISODEC). This and subsequent workshops were facilitated by a qualified engineer from this NGO. This individual wrote up and distributed all the points agreed in workshops.

By the end of this first workshop there was general agreement to go ahead with the implementation of the 8 standards which were not being met on the bridges project (child labour was not being used so was not relevant in this case).The next four workshops were held at 6 monthly intervals. They addressed specific implementation issues: problems were listed, discussed by all and a solution proposed. In the subsequent workshop stakeholders reported back on what they had done and whether the solution had 'worked'. These discussions were recorded by the NGO facilitator. The workshops were funded by DFID, hosted by the Department of Feeder Roads, and organised by the NGO. (Costs: 5 workshops @ US$4000 each, total $20,000 over 3 years)

Action Point 9. Identify which standards to focus on (community contracting and self-help schemes)

One of the perceived benefits of community contracting is the emphasis on implementation based on community priorities and inputs. However, there is often concern that compliance with nine labour standards will increase regulation and over-burden community capacity to deal with such issues.

Case studies have shown that while it is essential to assess the extent to which all nine labour standards have application in any particular community contracting context, in practice it may be necessary to initially address those standards identified and prioritised by communities. Some can be dealt with through informal local measures. For example, health and safety issues arise in all cases and need action, but local mechanisms of support can sometimes ensure that food, drinking water and sanitation facilities are provided for workers by the local community. However, if local mechanisms cannot be definitely relied upon then specific action will be required to ensure workers have access to these basic facilities.

With regard to unpaid work, the fact that a person offers to undertake unpaid work does not mean that they are offering to forego other labour rights. Whether unpaid work is legislated for or not, the dominant incentive for compliance is the local social relationships between those in charge of the infrastructure work and those providing labour. One of the worst things that can happen to a community undertaking a project on an unpaid basis is that one of its members has an accident.

In unpaid work there is need to review the application of <u>all</u> labour standards <u>except</u> those which apply to wages and to deliberate casualisation. The main labour standards that apply in unpaid labour schemes are:

- provision for social security. This is important in the event of serious accident, hence accident insurance should be considered;

- health and safety. This is critical; a way needs to be found of ensuring workers wear protective clothing for tasks requiring it. Skilled workers need to be bought in for jobs requiring specialist skills. There needs to be access to medical treatment for all workers and a means by which workers can pay for such treatment;

- no forced labour (explicit or implicit);

- agreement with community on working hours; and

- concerns around equality of treatment and child labour. These should be discussed with the community in advance, and appropriate measures taken.

Box 6 provides an overview of the issues that may arise during the identification stage and possible actions that can be taken during implementation. While it primarily relates to community contracting and unpaid self-help schemes, several of the issues have relevance for formal contracting also.

Box 6. Labour Standards in Community Contracting and Self-help Schemes		
Labour Standard	**The problem**	**Actions: What can be done?**
1. Freedom of Association and the effective recognition of the right to collective bargaining.	Trade unions usually not active in this unorganized sector.TUs are not found on many rural community contracting sites.	■ Be open to collective bargaining; recognise local informal groups that represent workers e.g. CBOs, NGOs, workers groups who can develop home-grown solutions. ■ Discuss mechanisms for implementing labour standards in advance of the work and seek their views on monitoring. ■ Establish transparent complaint and dispute resolution procedures.
2. The elimination of all forms of forces or compulsory labour.	In some self-help schemes, infrastructure can be denied unless labour is provided on an unpaid basis. Poor households (most often women) work for free while better off households can afford to give financial contributions.	■ Check that the agreement to provide unpaid labour is acceptable to the community at large, not just the leaders. ■ Ensure that there are exemptions for those deemed to be vulnerable e.g. pregnant women, aged, children of school going age, disabled, the poorest households, female headed households.

	Box 6. continued	
Labour Standard	**The problem**	**Actions: What can be done?**
3. **The effective abolition of child labour (under 15 years or country accepted minimum legal age applicable to the type of work).**	In poorest households or child headed households, children may be obliged to work.	■ Review practices that rely on child labour including those of sub-contractors. ■ Discuss options with parents/children (some may be child heads of households). ■ Pay a living wage to parents and children. ■ Review whether work interferes with education & restructure the tasks and the time. ■ Review all sources of materials to see if child labour is involved. ■ Be pro-active in reducing child labour, set priorities and establish an action plan towards its elimination without increasing poverty. ■ Monitor impact closely.
4. **The elimination of discrimination in respect of employment and occupation.**	Gender wage disparities endemic and institutionalized e.g. in PWD rates. Lack of opportunities for women and casual workers to become skilled construction workers reinforces unequal wages. Typically, there exists in-built bias against creating viable jobs for women or disabled workers in paid work.	■ Difficult to overcome entrenched biases: What does national/state legislation say? Make compliance a part of the contract. ■ Contract rates should specify equal wages. ■ Monitor muster roles. ■ May need to provide training to raise awareness among contractors/foremen. ■ Use women's groups/networks to communicate with women. ■ Try rotating traditional roles among men and women. ■ Build in skills training for women in basic engineering, construction and supervision. ■ Allocate tasks to groups of women who can organize the work amongst themselves to fit in with other responsibilities.

Box 6. continued		
Labour Standard	**The problem**	**Actions: What can be done?**
5. Health and Safety to be assured.	*Accident prevention* Community/self-help groups or petty contractors are not familiar with safety standards and labourers are primarily local unskilled workers.	■ Require a specific health and safety proposal at design stage which identifies potential hazards and risks and how they will be dealt with e.g. only skilled workers permitted to carry out risky tasks.
	Dealing with accidents Typically, no liability coverage so victims have to pay medical expenses and suffer income loss.	■ Prioritise accident prevention through awareness creation and training; focus on the concept of removing hazards and risk as a first step; provide protective clothing, first aid kits on site ■ Provide awareness training on risks and make provision for insurance/workmen's compensation and availability of first aid kit in project costs. Where possible, use health and safety competence as a criteria for choosing contractors. ■ Distinguish between minor and serious accidents: (i) minor accidents require an immediate response to deal with medical treatment and costs, and loss of income. (ii) serious accidents need additional provisions such as insurance against death, physical disablement.
	Protective clothing Low awareness of the need, and costs high relative to wages.	■ Create awareness of its importance.· Costs to be included in the works' budget. ■ Decide with the client and community on storage, maintenance and ownership.
	First Aid.	■ Establish safety committee and emergency procedures; nominate and train a safety officer and first aid person. Promote health education and HIV/AIDS awareness and prevention.

Box 6. continued

Labour Standard	The problem	Actions: What can be done?
	Amenities (drinking water, sanitation, food) Scale of works often preclude the formal provision for drinking water and sanitation.	■ As a majority of workers are usually local, drinking water and sanitation facilities may be accessed from neighbouring households. ■ Food may be provided by community members but if not, it will be necessary to provide amenities as a cost item.
6. **Wages to be paid in full and on time, to meet legal minima, and be sufficient for basic needs.**	Wages are often set low because of a surplus of labour, resulting in difficulties for workers to support themselves. Minimum wages are often well below market rates. Wages paid late because contractor hasn't the cash flow and the client does not pay in time.	■ Assess minimum wage (or Public Works Department rate) to see its relevance. ■ Set a realistic wage for casuals and permanent workers that supports people's livelihoods and monitor muster rolls i.e. provide a LIVING WAGE. ■ Be transparent in setting wage rates and keep register of payments or provide wage slips. ■ Pay wages on time – poor people cannot extend credit lines.
7. **Working hours to be limited; overtime to be paid.**	Workers can be obliged to work long hours, especially if the contract includes a penalty clause for delays. In self-help schemes, workers may have little influence over how long they work. The requirement to do additional work may conflict with other livelihood strategies.	■ Keep work records and monitor *with the* worker. ■ Create additional jobs rather than increasing the workload of existing workers. ■ Set task rates with reasonable time. ■ Review management and supervision of works. ■ Discuss with the community and workers the scheduling of work such that it facilitates workers' other responsibilities.

Box 6. continued		
Labour Standard	**The problem**	**Actions: What can be done?**
8. No repeated casualisation to avoid meeting wages and other legal benefits; equality of treatment for casuals.	Casual workers not treated equally because they are usually unskilled – wages lower and no social security.	■ Pay a fair wage. In the absence of other safety nets, prioritise accident insurance.
9. All relevant social security regimes to be applied.	Difficulties in bringing irregular casual workers into social security nets/accident insurance. Community groups don't have accident coverage or other social security provision.	■ Explore possibilities for coverage under existing social security schemes; if casual workers cannot be covered an accident insurance scheme will be necessary, especially for serious accidents. ■ Make provision within the project/at local level to deal with minor accidents quickly e.g. create a fund.

Action Point 10. How can workers realise their rights if they are employed on a temporary basis - or in self-help schemes?

In most developing countries the majority of workers are employed on a temporary basis even in formal contracting. Only a small percentage of the total construction workforce in a country comprise 'permanent' employees who are also registered for social security. The majority, whether they work in formal and community contracting or in self-help schemes are 'temporary' workers.[14]

---

[14] In the formal contracting sector the 'temporary' category normally includes at least two categories of worker. These are, firstly, 'casuals', i.e. those employed on a specific project, on daily wages, for specific, unskilled tasks. This group are likely to live locally and work as construction labourers to supplement other livelihood strategies (e.g. in agriculture). A second group are those we might refer to as 'permanent casuals'. In Ghana this group included both skilled and unskilled workers who defined their main occupation as 'construction', had many years of experience - often for the same employer - but had never been registered by any of their employers for social security.

A major issue in construction works is whether and how these temporary workers can receive benefits on a par with permanent (and registered) workers. In practice, temporary workers, who are mostly unskilled and amongst the poorest, neither receive the benefits of permanent workers nor additional wage rates to compensate for the loss of benefits.

In most countries, national legislation does not provide for temporary workers, however defined. Nor are social security systems designed for workers who can contribute only sporadically; in most countries both the employer and the worker must contribute continuously for 20 (or so) years before qualifying for the main benefit: a pension. In the absence of schemes which take account of the temporal nature of most employment the temporary worker tends to be discriminated against several times over. For example, most temporary workers are paid less than permanents, yet if injured - perhaps due to a lack of safety equipment or protective clothing on site which may be provided to permanents - they must pay for medical treatment themselves; in the meantime they get no compensation for loss of income. As a category of worker they are therefore extremely vulnerable.

What can be done will vary according to the local context. However, in general:

√ Review the benefits enjoyed by all workers, and compare the benefits that permanent workers get with those of different categories of temporary worker. Equality of treatment is a key labour standard and workers should not be discriminated against because they are casual workers. Factors to be taken into account are the regularity of work, the nature of the task, and the skill involved.

√ Health and safety provisions should be common for all.

√ If the construction works continue for a sustained period of time (the legal limit for casual work) then labourers should be registered for social security entitlements.

√ In the case of serious accidents, where it is not possible to bring casual unskilled workers under the state social security system, accident insurance will need to be provided to pay for disability, death, serious medical expenses and loss of income.

√ The best option for dealing with minor accidents in community contracting may be the creation of some form of local fund that can respond quickly to meet medical expenses as the bureaucracy in most insurance companies is a deterrent to claiming small amounts of compensation, especially by the less educated.

C. Implementing labour standards

The following steps are necessary to implement a labour standards programme. These activities need to take place in parallel:

- develop and budget for a consultation process;

- anticipate the concerns of stakeholders;

- incorporate labour standards in contract documents;

- cost each labour standard and agree who will pay;

- ensure communities and workers are informed about their rights; and

- build capacity.

Action Points 11- 16 are included in this "Implementing labour standards" section.

Action Point 11. Develop - and budget for - a consultation process

A number of parties have roles to play in implementing labour standards. They are more likely to co-operate if they know exactly what is going on, and have a chance to voice their concerns.

√ Plan and budget for a programme of stakeholder workshops to address implementation issues. The importance of such workshops cannot be overemphasised - they will be the main mechanism for checking progress, discussing problems and agreeing future action.

√ Plan and budget for training and briefing sessions for specific groups. Training is needed for contractors and separately, for employers and supervising engineers. (Further ideas on the substance of these sessions is given in action point 13 on building capacity).

√ Plan and budget for discussion and awareness raising sessions for workers and communities. (Also discussed later - see action point 16 on ensuring communities are informed about their rights).

See Box 8 under action point 15 for the different sort of costs - including consultation workshop and training costs - associated with implementing each labour standard in the Ghana study.

Action Point 12. Anticipate the concerns of stakeholders

√ Anticipate the concerns of different stakeholders as much as possible. Labour standards will be a completely new idea to most of them. They will inevitably have reservations. Some of the difficulties voiced in the Ghana programme are listed in Box 7 below. All the issues were eventually resolved.

√ Community contracts are more informal in nature than in the formal contracting sector and tend to focus on the construction activity. Little thought is usually given to labour standards or to the rights, responsibilities and liabilities of different parties. Without the 'incentive' of a formal contract to get people involved success in promoting labour standards will tend to depend on people's good will and preparedness to 'buy in' to the activity. In these circumstances dissemination and awareness raising of labour issues must become an integral part of the project process. For example, disseminating the findings of the baseline survey to stakeholders can be an important vehicle to raise issues around labour standards and to generate support. It can help:

- the development of a broad base for feedback on emerging issues;
- define actions needed to be taken at various levels;
- identify changes needed in the legal/regulatory/procedural framework;
- identify subsequent responsibilities and gauge capacity to meet these responsibilities;
- help to target specific dissemination activities; and
- help to up-scale labour standards generally.

Box 7.   Initial concerns of stakeholders: and suggested action

Stakeholder	Possible Concerns	Suggested action
1. The client (e.g. Ministry of Roads, Public Works).	■ May have several concerns, e.g. over timescale of works, extra costs, 'rabble raising' by workers, more burdens for emerging contractors.	■ Put time into developing a relationship with the client; be ready to go at their pace; their support is essential. ■ Be conversant with labour law - stress the programme will help the department fulfil their regulatory obligations. ■ Be ready with examples of how it has worked elsewhere - of timescale and costs, of productivity gains, of capacity development for contractors. ■ Encourage the client to see the benefits of taking part in a initiative involving global players, e.g. the ILO, the World Bank, relevant donors.
2. Engineers working for the Employer (e.g. Ministry of Roads).	■ May not feel labour standards is their responsibility; see their role as purely technical. ■ May have difficulties with particular standards, e.g. may see gender as a cultural issue and HIV/AIDS irrelevant to their role as engineers.	■ Ensure that labour standards is supported by the top of the department or ministry - this will legitimise it for staff. ■ Bring engineers into contact with other stakeholders so they have a chance to see issues from different points of view. ■ Over time you can anticipate that their interest will increase - they will begin to see labour standards work as extending their skills, and their status.
3. Supervising Engineers/ Employers' Representatives.	■ Concerns as for Employer. ■ May resist adding monitoring labour standards to their technical monitoring role. ■ May see this as an additional job for which they are unqualified and/or want to be paid.	■ Action as above. ■ Build labour standard monitoring into the terms of reference for contract supervision. Include this in the service contract between the engineer and client. Stress the need for SEs to be committed to the programme, otherwise they will be poor monitors (as they would rather be doing the engineering). ■ Specific training on labour standards will be required. Once familiar with the issues, the issue of additional pay may die away.

Box 7.   continued

Stakeholder	Possible Concerns	Suggested action
4. Association of Contrac- tors - and individual contractors.	Likely to be the most resistant group and to have a range of questions, e.g. ■ who will pay? - will insist standards be paid for by the employer. ■ how to procure labour standard items (e.g. protective clothing) and transport to distant sites? ■ who will do the record keeping? ■ trade union visits may incite workers. ■ will there be rewards for compliance? ■ will there be sanctions for non compli- ance? ■ HIV/AIDS not their concern.	■ Involve contractors as much as possible in initial planning discussions. ■ Ensure - as a result of total commit- ment from the Employer - that the implementation of labour standards will be a bid assessment criterion. ■ Ensure the client has made it clear to contractors that they will not have to pay for standards from their overheads (e.g. by including labour items in BoQ where necessary). ■ Provide detailed specifications so that contractors are clear about what the requirements are. If the bidders are inexperienced in pricing for labour standards include PC sums in the BOQ. ■ Explain labour standards at all pre-bid meetings using well-prepared materials which potential bidders can take away. ■ Arrange briefing/training sessions at award of contract so that all know their roles and responsibilities. ■ Ensure contractors are clear about what will be monitored so they brief their site representatives. ■ Get contractors and unions together to talk about their common interests. ■ Reward compliance. (In Ghana an additional 10% of the engineer's estimated budget for labour standards implementation was paid to those contractors who were deemed by the Employer to have implemented them effectively).
5. Ministry of Labour (department responsible for labour inspections).	■ Will support the labour standards programme but may not have the resources to visit and inspect sites.	■ Agree with the department whether it is feasible for them to be involved, and if so how. ■ Invite to all stakeholder workshops so they can keep abreast of progress and provide information and advice on labour law and good practice.

Box 7.   continued

Stakeholder	Possible Concerns	Suggested action
6. The trade unions for the sector.	■ May not have the capacity (staff) or resources (transport, running costs), to play an active role outside the major towns, particularly if the number of workers on site is small.	■ Be prepared to ask the funding agency for additional resources for the trade unions (e.g. transport, training) if requested. Otherwise trade unions may not be able to help with two vital jobs: raising worker awareness, and monitoring the implementation of labour standards on sites.
7. Dept of Social Security and National Insurance.	■ May see the project as a way of getting more people to register (so will be supportive).	■ No general guidance possible as it depends on national law. In principle, registering is to be encouraged as a social safety net for all workers. But if the law stipulates a 20 year contribution to qualify for a pension it will be difficult to convince temporary workers to register (and contractors may not encourage them to register as they will want to minimise the amount they pay in employer contributions).

Box 7.	continued	
Stakeholder	**Possible Concerns**	**Suggested action**
8. Workers - permanent and daily wage - and adjacent communities.	■ Workers likely to prioritise pay above every other standard - at least initially. ■ At first, may not like wearing protective clothing, may sell it. May not see the point of latrines; may be wary of unions; may not want women on site; may prefer to side with contractor for fear of losing job.	■ Plan a programme of worker and community education. In Ghana this was achieved through visits to communities and discussion with workers by the trade union and NGO - and eventually through the support of supervising engineers and regular site meetings. ■ Anticipate initial wariness but increasing support for labour standards by workers. Anticipate that the word will spread and they will begin to lobby other contractors for standards, particularly increased wages, protective clothing, potable water.
9. Other donors (bilateral and multilateral donors and finance institutions).	■ Likely to be interested but to have limited experience unless gained through involvement with ILO labour intensive infrastructure programme.	■ Target donors funding the same employer/line department. ■ Ensure a consistent donor approach to labour standards. Avoid burdening the ministry with requests for slightly different standards or procedures. ■ Get the Employer (ministry) to ask other donors to apply the same standards. This is by far the best way to galvanise other donors to act.

Action point 13. Build the capacity of stakeholders to implement labour standards

Capacity building is one of the most important components of any labour standards scheme and an essential criterion for success. The point at which capacity building is needed is obvious in formal contracting but less clear in community contracting and self help schemes.

In formal contracting:

√ Include Labour Standard briefings in all *Pre-Bid Meetings*. Materials for pre-bid meetings need to be prepared (in hand-out form as well as on charts or overheads) and should cover:

- what the labour standards are and their relationship to national law;

- the business benefits for contractors in implementing labour standards;

- where labour standards will be addressed in the conditions of contract and associated specifications;

- how they should cost each standard in their bid;

- who will monitor implementation on site; and

- any incentives agreed for compliance - or sanctions for non-compliance.

√ Organise training on labour standards at, or following, the *Award of Contract meeting*. Training should cover:

- all the issues listed above under pre-bid meeting;

- the record keeping system and how this will work (if this is new). Note that if records have not been kept by contractors before then proforma need to be given out at this meeting and all made aware of exactly how they should be filled in;

- the way in which contractors and site managers should interact with unions (if relevant);

- the monitoring indicators (i.e. the checks to be made by the Supervising Engineers or other monitoring group); and

- the fact that progress towards compliance with labour standards as agreed will be a regular agenda item at site meetings.

√ Hold *training sessions for engineers*: both line department staff and their Representatives (*Supervising Engineers*). It is likely that SEs will have full or part responsibility for monitoring - it is therefore very important they understand them. Cover all the issues as for contractors. SEs will also need a list of monitoring indicators, i.e. a checklist of what they should be looking out for.

√ In all interactions create a climate where all parties - Contractors, Employers and Supervising Engineers - see themselves as joint partners in piloting labour standards work. Acknowledge and spend time on any of their concerns.

In community contracting and self-help schemes:
Community groups or petty contractors, who manage implementation of community contracts, are often unaware of the obligation to meet labour standards, and lack the capacity to do so.

√ Introduce discussions on labour standards from the design stage of the project so that key challenges can be taken account of, planned for, and costed.

√ Awareness creation and training is critical to changing social perceptions of the need and value of complying with labour standards, and should be provided and targeted specifically at the needs and interests of particular groups. The chart below provides a guide to the training that may be required by the different stakeholders.

Possible training requirements of stakeholders in community contracting and self-help schemes are:

Target Group	Awareness raising	Implementation processes	Monitoring
Local authority	✓	✓	✓
Labour Department (if relevant)	✓	✓	✓
Community-based organisation	✓	✓	✓
Contractors/petty and sub-contractors	✓	✓	✓
Citizens	✓		
Workers	✓	✓	✓
NGO/Trade union or other representative association	✓	✓	✓
Funders	✓		✓
Technical officers	✓	✓	

The modules should address all nine labour standards and draw attention to those that have particular application to the project and location (e.g. health and safety, wages and social security). In addition training will need to cover:

- equality of treatment: participation and treatment of women, casuals, migrants, disabled, aged, HIV/AIDS workers;

- costs of each standard it is decided to implement - not just protective measures/ garments;

- procurement - where, and by whom;

- prevention and support measures proposed around HIV/AIDS;

- incentives/enforcement for compliance; and

- monitoring indicators - how and by whom monitoring will be done.

Action point 14.   Incorporate labour standards in contract documents (formal contracting) and community contracting agreements

Formal contracting

There are a number of different documents which form part of the contract and consideration needs to be given to the implications of labour standard implementation. For example, FIDIC clause 5.2 refers to, in order of precedence:

- The Contract Agreement: that is, "an agreement between the two parties to the contract based upon a definite offer by one of the parties and an unqualified acceptance of the offer by the other party"

- The letter of acceptance, defined as "the formal acceptance by the employer of the tender, which forms the contract between the employer and the contractor"

- The tender, defined as "the contractor's priced offer to the employer for the execution and completion of the works and the remedying of any defects therein in accordance with the provisions of the contract, as accepted by the Letter of Acceptance". The costs of labour standards and the different options for including them within the contractual and bidding framework are considered separately in action points 15 and18.

- Part 2 Conditions of Particular Application (see below)

- Part 1 General Conditions (see below)

- Any other documents forming part of the contract (see below)

The review of a number of different conditions of contract in relation to labour standards is described in action point 2. This review together with a listing of contract clause wording is presented in Part 3 of the sourcebook. With the exception of the "DFID Interim Guidelines", all of the clauses have actually been used and tested in practice.

The following steps assist in the process of implementation through contract claues.

√ Refer back to the outcome of action point 8 which identifies which labour standards to focus on in formal contracting.

√ In the first instance, try to identify suitable clauses from Part 3.

√ In general, DO NOT propose any changes to General Conditions of Contract.

√ If you need to insert additional clauses, do so in the Special Conditions or Conditions of Particular Application.

√ If you insert any new clauses in to the Special Conditions which have not been used before in those circumstances, it is advisable to take legal advice in order to ensure that no ambiguity is created with either the General Conditions or the other clauses in the Special Conditions. There may be unforeseen "knock-on" effects.

√ The other documents which form part of the contract offer the opportunity to provide much more operational detail. One of the difficulties of introducing labour standards is that both employer and contractor will need to work out the details of what to do. Remember that contract clauses often express an intention to do something: for example "to take due precautions, to ensure the safety of staff, to ensure that first aid equipment is available" etc. This is all very well, but it does not tell either the contractor or the employer what actually has to be done. The detail is important: for example, what safety equipment is required? what should be the contents of a first aid box? These operational details are key to the overall success of implementing labour standards in order that they can be accurately costed and monitored for compliance.

√ Box 19 in Part 3 provides a checklist of items to assist in developing a specification for the implementation of each of the nine labour standards. The specification needs to be reviewed for each separate contract, as the operational details will normally be location specific. The specification for labour standards can then be included as part of the contract documents and be legally enforced through the contract. Care needs to be taken in situations where neither employer nor contractor are experienced in labour standards. The importance of the participative process is crucial (see action points 8, 12 and 13).

Community contracting agreements[15]

Unlike formal or conventional contracting, there is no generalised framework for community contracting. The underlying principles are as follows:

√ Depending on the context, set out clearly the contractual relationships and responsibility. While verbal agreements are legally binding and labour standards can be incorporated as conditions in any type of agreement, it is preferable to have a written agreement, as it may not be practical to incorporate nine labour standards within a verbal agreement.

√ In some situations the best option may be to seek to influence government procedures such that they tackle labour standards, in others, voluntary buy-in will be the determining factor.

√ If a contract has already been agreed and is under implementation, it will be necessary to review the social clauses in the existing contract. If these are considered inadequate, with mutual agreement, a supplementary agreement or variation can be negotiated.

√ Useful entry points to include labour standards within existing works are annual reviews, revision of logframes, or revision of terms of reference.

Action Point 15. Determine the cost of implementing labour standards and agree who will pay

There are four important issues regarding the cost of labour standards:

■ Issue 1: The direct and indirect financial costs of implementing labour standards

■ Issue 2: Agreeing who will pay these costs

---

[15] Detailed cases of community contracts, including the range of roles and responsibilities taken on by community groups, are given in "Community Initiatives in Urban Infrastructure" by A P Cotton, M Sohail and W K Tayler (available from WEDC, Loughborough University www.lboro.ac.uk/wedc/ Also see "Community contracts in urban infrastructure works. Practical lessons from experience". Tournee, J., and W van Esch, ILO Geneva 2000".

- Issue 3: Additional issues to consider in pricing (formal contracting)
- Issue 4: Additional issues to consider in pricing (community contracting)

Issue 1. The direct and indirect financial costs of implementing labour standards

These generally include:

- protective measures e.g. clothing;
- basic services provided such as water supply and sanitation;
- social security;
- insurance costs (premiums will come down if best practice is applied);
- capacity building, consultation, facilitation and promotion costs;
- equality opportunity costs; and
- transactional costs including dialogue and monitoring.

Use the checklist in Box 19 in Part 3 for guidance concerning the specific items likely to be associated with the different labour standards.

Box 8 looks at the nature of the costs associated with each labour standard in a formal contracting context (although many points are also relevant to community contracting and self-help schemes). Box 9 gives an example of how these costs were estimated in the Ghana study. It shows that some cost items can be estimated but flexibility needs to be built into the labour standards budget so that there is provision to respond to issues as they arise.

Box 8.   Costs associated with each labour standard

Labour standard	Type of cost (using Ghana pilot as an example)
1. The right of workers to freedom of association, and to bargain collectively.	In order to exercise this right, workers need physical access to a Trade Union. In many countries this is automatic and has no cost. But in Ghana, because some sites were 500 km from the nearest union office and the TU had no vehicle, DFID provided the Trade Union with transport costs so they could physically get to sites and interact with workers. This had a cost to the donor and to the Union (the opportunity cost of visiting far flung rural sites).
2. No discrimination.	Again there are normally no costs associated with this standard. However, in Ghana, because no record keeping was done there was no way of recording the gender or other characteristic of the workers. A record system was therefore set up - and this had a cost (e.g. the part-time services of a record keeper). But because contractors found this useful they agreed to adopt it as standard practice. Where women are systematically denied job opportunities and the chance to develop skills there will be costs if it is decided to fund training courses specifically for them. In Ghana DANIDA (Danish International Development Agency) is funding a technical and supervisory course for women construction workers to enable them to more effectively compete for supervisory positions. This is an example of an extremely useful complimentary activity by another donor.
3. No forced labour.	No direct costs. But again, record keeping is required to monitor the working hours of workers.
4. No child labour.	No costs in Ghana because not relevant. However, if the project had decided to address child labour in the supply chain (aggregate making where there is child labour) then there would have been considerable costs. It would have meant another agency (not DFR) providing child care or even education for children on site. The loss of the income to the family group would also have had to be addressed.

Note: where child labour exists then the Employer should get help from other partners. The issues are complex and it is not just a case of forbidding women to bring their children to a site. This can result in discriminating against them. The ILO office should be the first point of contact for advice on how to deal with child labour. |

Box 8. continued	
Labour standard	**Type of cost (using Ghana pilot as an example)**
5. Health and safety to be addressed.	Most health and safety items have direct costs that the contractors can price. For example: protective clothing (standard for all workers and that required for special tasks); tanks for potable water (the water may or may not have a cost depending on source); first aid kit (items to be specified by the Employer); latrines (according to a specification provided by the Employer). The formation of a safety committee and time off for it to meet will be an indirect cost/overhead. Workmen's Compensation may only apply to permanent workers and thus accident insurance should be costed for all workers.
6. Wages to be paid in full and on time, to meet legal minima and be sufficient for basic needs.	If contractors are paying below the legal minima and/or that defined in Collective Agreements then paying the minimum wage as a result of labour standard implementation will increase the contractor's bid price. The Employer will need to take this into account when assessing bids and not go for 'the lowest bid' if it is clear that the bidder has not adequately reflected labour costs - including adequate wages - in the bid price. Where line ministry rates are being used in the costing, recognise that these may be out of date and require upward adjustment. Parity of wages for men and women should be reflected in the costing. In Kerala, Public Works Dept rates were well below market rates, and reinforced gender disparity by paying women much less than men.
7. Working hours to be limited; overtime to be paid.	Overtime will have a direct cost for contractors, and they will need to reflect the likelihood of this in their bids. Pay records should record overtime and provide a means of checking that the contractor does not move to task-based work if this is against the stipulations of the contract.
8. No repeated casualisation to avoid meeting wages and other legal benefits.	Regularising long term casuals will have a cost. The contractor must budget for additional social security contributions (12% of salary in Ghana) and this will then be reflected in the bid price. Again, the Employer will need to take this into account when assessing bids.
9. All relevant social security regimes to be applied.	Budget for social security contributions for all workers, as above.
10.HIV/AIDS to be addressed.	HIV/AIDS awareness sessions have a cost; so also do the purchase of condoms (if it is decided to do this). However, funding might be available from elsewhere. In Ghana there is provision for sector ministries to apply for funds from a central HIV/AIDS budget.

Box 9. Estimating costs: how possible is this? An example from Ghana

1. *Health and safety items.* It is possible to estimate the cost of (a) building latrines and (b) protective clothing. In Ghana, on bridges sites of between 15-20 operatives, the cost of providing general protective clothing (boots, overalls, helmets and gloves) and clothing for specific tasks (raincoat, rubber boots, dust mask, safety goggles and ear defenders) was between 2-3% of project costs.

2. *Stakeholder Workshops:* Also possible to estimate. In Ghana, five residential 2-3 day workshops were held over 3 years, with approximately 30 participants each time. Each workshop cost approximately US $4000).

3. *Development of briefing/training materials* for: (a) engineers (b) contractors (c) the monitors. Costs will depend on who develops these materials. In Ghana the NGO that helped with implementation and monitoring was commissioned to prepare these materials in collaboration with DFR. The trade union was also funded to provide guidelines on the international labour standards and the rights of workers under Ghana national law. In Kerala, they were developed by the NGO with the Labour Dept.

4. *Training sessions on labour standards for engineers.* Costs depend on the numbers of engineers involved.

5. *Briefing sessions for contractors* at pre-bid meetings and at award. Costs depend on the number of contracts to be let.

6. *Monitoring visits to sites.* Costs include fee days, transport and accommodation costs for any members of the monitoring team who would not otherwise make these visits.

7. *Awareness raising for communities.* Costs depend on the geographical spread of the physical works, the number of visits it is decided to make, and the accessibility of communities who will be providing labour.

8. *Impact evaluation study* to assess the impact on livelihoods of workers before completion of the programme. Costs depend on the scope of the study.

Issue 2. Agreeing who will pay

In formal contracting the increased costs associated with improved labour standards will be paid for by the employer through higher bid prices from contractors. Eventually, when the incorporation of labour standards becomes commonplace, we would expect contractors to be familiar with the requirements and to improve their own efficiency to absorb some of the costs in order to increase their competitiveness in bidding. However, this was not within the scope of (and therefore not demonstrated by) this study.

Technical assistance funding from donors is likely to be important during the early stages of setting up and mainstreaming improved labour standards. For example, the role played by DFID in monitoring in the Ghana case.

In community contracting and self-help schemes costs should be included in the project costs – it is not reasonable to assume that the community can absorb such costs as part of its contribution. Experience in Kerala demonstrated that while there may be other budget lines available to communities under decentralisation for its activities, in practice these proved difficult to access in a timely manner. The Kerala experience also showed that there can be significant economies of scale if the State is involved e.g. negotiating with insurance companies, otherwise the costs may be high for an individual community.

Issue 3. Additional issues to consider in pricing (formal contracting)
It is important that the pricing of labour standards in competitive bids is realistic, otherwise there will be problems during implementation. Where there is little or no experience of bringing in labour standards, then both the employer and the contractor will need technical support throughout the competitive bidding process to ensure that the prices are adequate to meet the needs. This is illustrated by the approaches tried out in Ghana with varying amounts of success. An iterative process was followed there, as follows:

1. Initially, contractor-priced labour standards items were included in the Bill of Quantities. However, it was clear during an early bid evaluation that many of the bidders had no idea what they were pricing for and consequently the rates were very low. This gave problems during the construction period.

2. For the second batch of contracts the labour standards items were put in as prime cost sums, priced by the engineer. However, during implementation it became clear that:
   - the rates were not sufficient to cover the actual costs for procuring various items; and

   - administering these prime cost sums was very difficult as receipts and invoices have to be obtained to support all expenditure. For example, receipts are very easy to obtain for protective clothing from a shop, but very difficult /impossible for supplies of tubewell water from a local community.

3. Finally, in the third batch of contracts, an attempt was made to improve on the specification of the items which helped to alleviate pricing problems experi-

enced in 1 and 2 above. This is where the checklist in Box 19 Part 3 can be very useful.

Experience suggests that time and effort needs to be put in by the employer in order to specify the costs as clearly as possible, and to include these as prime cost items. When there is greater familiarity of requirements on both sides it should be possible to move towards the contractor-based pricing through the Bill of Quantities.

It is very important to discuss pricing of labour standards at the pre-bid meetings (see action point 13), when potential bidders will be advised that the inclusion of labour standards will be taken into account during bid appraisal.

Issue 4. Additional issues to consider in pricing (community contracting)

In situations where community contracting is well established, contracts are sometimes let on a competitive basis, in which case the points made in Issue 3 above will apply. However, it is far more common for work to be entrusted to a community group without bidding. Part of the support to the community contracting process relates to budgeting and cost control and it is essential that the employer and community contractor include the necessary costs to cover what has been agreed in terms of labour standards. (See also action point 9). This also applies to unwaged voluntary work.

In general:

√ Implementing labour standards should be incorporated within the construction project plan budget, and this should be a criteria for project approval.

√ If the project is already under implementation, it is unlikely that provision for such costs has been made in the project budget and no action will be taken. In community contracting, which may have a long timescale, it may be realistic to bring in simple interim measures. For example, small additional funds can be made available to purchase protective clothing/first aid kits, or insurance.

√ Investing in an insurance policy may be the only way to protect casual workers, in the event of death, physical disablement or expensive medical treatment.

√ If an insurance scheme is required, it may be cost effective to negotiate at a provincial or State level, otherwise the premium will be too high for community groups to insure a small number of workers.

Action Point 16. Ensure communities and workers are informed about their rights

Labour standards will be as new for workers and communities as they are for engineers. It is important that they are made aware of the rights and benefits that they are entitled to, and where necessary, the underlying reasons for these.

√ Agree who will be responsible for worker and community awareness raising.

√ Plan an awareness/education strategy in collaboration with relevant stakeholders.

√ Get representatives of stakeholder groups to visit communities/sites. For example, a trade union representative to explain about trade unions; someone from the department of social security to talk about social security; someone from the department of health (or other relevant body) to talk about protection from HIV/AIDs. (However, where the relevant bodies are not available, individuals equipped with the relevant basic information can also undertake these tasks).

√ Use visual examples to explain standards. For example, if protective clothing is to be provided, take examples of each item. If records are to be kept, take the record forms. (If there is electricity consider showing the SAC video on labour standards in Ghana to prompt discussion).

√ Anticipate some initial problems. In Ghana, a pair of wellington boots is equivalent to a month's wage so the inclination to sell them at times of emergency is strong. So also is the tendency to keep overalls and steel capped boots for best. If a good consultative relationship has been built between workers and contractors (more usually, site representatives and foremen) then there is much greater likelihood that these issues can be discussed and resolved at a site level.

√ Ensure there is a systematic way for workers to contribute to site meetings. The implementation and monitoring of labour standards is about providing decent work for workers, including temporary workers. They must be able to say whether labour standards are being implemented in such a way as to achieve this. They are also best placed to advise on how to deal with specific problems (e.g. distress sales of protective clothing).

D. Monitoring labour standards

Action point 17. Monitor for compliance

As highlighted previously, labour standards are not implemented mainly because they are not monitored. The development of a robust monitoring system, with clear roles and responsibilities for carrying out the monitoring task is essential. Labour standard implementation must be monitored and must be seen to be monitored. Incentives and sanctions play a part in monitoring because contractors (both conventional and community) are unlikely to implement the required standards unless they see a benefit to themselves in doing so (or a penalty in their failure). Monitoring systems should be agreed and put in place before the physical works start.

√ Decide who will be responsible for monitoring and how they will report on this. See Box 10 for how this worked in the formal sector in Ghana.

Box 10. Monitoring compliance in Ghana

In Ghana it was initially agreed that a monitoring team would comprise:

- DFR Engineers
- the Supervising Engineers (SEs)
- the Trade Union (CBMWU)
- the Department of Labour
- the facilitating NGO (ISODEC)

It was agreed that the monitors would make unannounced visits to sites so that they could observe labour standards as they were normally applied.

But there were problems. Neither the trade union nor the Department of Labour had a vehicle so they could not get to sites. DFID offered to help with transport costs but no taxi would travel from Accra. Rates for 4 wheel drive vehicles were prohibitive. The problem was partially solved when the trade union officer began to travel to sites with DFR Engineers. But this was not ideal as the Engineers had their own work to do on site and it was not always possible for the Union to spend sufficient time with workers.

Over time - and when a number of different monitoring approaches had been tried - Supervising Engineers began to take over the role of monitors. At first there was resistance from them but gradually - after a year of discussion and experimentation - they began to see this as part of their normal work.

Every site meeting now has a labour standards slot when the record system is checked and any other problems regarding labour standard implementation are discussed and sorted out. Members of the monitoring team attend as many site meetings as they can.

Use relevant monitoring mechanisms to check the implementation of each stand-ard mentioned in the contract:

√ Use *visual monitoring* to check that workers are using protective clothing for the job intended; women are not being sidelined into only one type of job; potable water is available; the latrine is built to specification and is clean; food is accessible; the record system is working, and so on.

√ Use the *record system* to check who is employed and for what duration, working hours, schedule of work for the day, pay, accidents, social security, tax and union dues, etc.

√ Use *conversations with workers* to cross check all the above. This is essential.

√ Discuss any inconsistencies with site agents and/or contractors at regular site meetings.

The site meeting will be the main mechanism for sorting out problems.

√ Agree how to deal with consistent non-compliance by a contractor. This can be done through incentives and/or sanctions. The incentives and sanctions adopted will depend on the type of contract (formal or community) and the local context. Some possible options are discussed further in action point 18.

Action point 18. Consider introducing incentives and sanctions

Again there is a difference between formal and community contracting with respect to incentives and sanctions.

In formal contracting there can be:

■ *Financial incentives.* An amount set aside in the contract (for example, 5-10% of the cost of labour standards stated in the bid) for compliance with all labour standards, to be drawn down on completion of the physical works and after agreement by monitors. (This is the current system in Ghana).

■ *Points awarded to contractors* that apply labour standards on their sites. Points so awarded are then taken into formal account (along with price and other standard award criteria) in future bidding processes.

Sanctions can be:

■ *Disqualification* from bidding for future contracts (or the next contract).

- *Financial sanctions.* For example, non-payment for a labour standard item that has not been implemented. In Ghana this was tried only after it was established that most contractors could and did comply but a few were not bothering to take the issue seriously (mainly the larger contractors). Thus, financial sanctions were only applied after it had been established that this did not constitute an 'unreasonable condition'.

- *Social pressure* from stakeholders. When non-compliance is discussed publicly at site meetings by the Employer and Supervising Engineers, contractors can feel under pressure to comply with labour standards.

√ Consider using a combination of incentives and sanctions, e.g. a financial incentive plus social pressure. Be prepared to disqualify contractors who continually ignore labour standards and flout contracts despite pre-bid and award briefings, discussion at site meetings etc.

√ Ensure that if 'labour standards compliance' is introduced as a criterion for award of contracts in future then this is done in a transparent manner. All contractors need to be fully informed about how labour standard compliance is assessed and how points are awarded.

In community contracting the problem is different. There is no formal enforcement body of labour standards, and penalties are not usually part of community contracts. Thus incentives for compliance are less clear, and must be of an informal nature.

√ The major incentive for addressing labour standards is the promotion and maintenance of good social relations, and ensuring that community members are not disadvantaged. For example, the negative impact of a serious accident on a community project where one's neighbour is severely injured, should not be under-estimated. The potential loss of social (or political) status by those with responsibility also functions as a strong disincentive to non-compliance.

√ Because the construction work is being carried out in conjunction with, and to the benefit of the community, it should be normal practice to work out an approach through discussion and dialogue with the various stakeholders which achieves best practice while enabling the construction work to proceed effectively and efficiently.

√ At a project level, some of the benefits of compliance are reduced number of accidents, better attendance, better time-project management, improved productivity, and healthier workforce.

√ Some recognition of best practice might also be considered.

Action Point 19. Monitor the impact of standards on workers and communities

It is important to monitor the impact of standards on workers for two reasons:

- to ensure that labour standard implementation really is having a positive effect on workers (and there are no unforeseen negative impacts); and

- to build up worker awareness of their rights so that they can form an upward pressure group for labour standard implementation when they work for other contractors.

In Zambia, monitoring demonstrated that the burden of unpaid work was falling to women, and the burden was such that they were not able to engage in income earning activities. Thus, there was a risk that the project was undermining rather than enhancing livelihoods. The project changed to paying workers, and only then did men participate.

√ Involve workers and communities in *monthly monitoring*. For example by agreeing to meet selected workers each month (men and women) to discuss which labour standards are being implemented, which are not, and what the impacts are.

√ Disaggregate impacts for women/men, permanent/casual, skilled/unskilled, migrants/locals, poorest/less poor.

√ Track compliance and breaches, and how these were dealt with so that they feed into further training.

√ Monitor accidents and their cause, and the extent of their seriousness; document how the project responded in terms of treatment, payment for treatment, compensation of the worker for loss of income.

√ Document grievances and mechanisms for resolution.

√ Undertake an *impact evaluation* of labour standards on workers and their communities once the programme is well underway but before it draws to a close. Box 11 describes how this is to be carried out in Ghana.

It is useful to have done a baseline survey as discussed in action point 5 and Appendix 1, as this will have recorded the situation before the project started.

Box 11. Impact evaluation in Ghana

In Ghana an impact evaluation of labour standards on the Bridges project will soon be commissioned. It will involve an assessment, by men and women workers, of:

- how much they now know about the working conditions they are entitled to;
- which labour standards are most important to them and why;
- what the impact of labour standards has been for them to date; and
- suggestions they would make to improve the labour standards programme.

Ad hoc reporting to date suggests the evaluation may show up some unusual findings. For example, that provision of boots and overalls is appreciated because of the status these give; the importance for women of being taken on for a wider range of construction tasks; the desire for a social security fund, even amongst casuals.

E. Institutionalising labour standards

Action Point 20. Scaling up: from project to programme to sector

√ Don't scale up until you have developed robust systems for implementation and monitoring labour standards in a pilot project.

√ Ensure that the experience gained in the pilot is in replicable form. To be replicable there need to be:
- well documented, easy to reproduce, briefing notes for contractors (for pre bid and award meetings) and training materials for engineers and monitors;

- agreement about who will take responsibility for a) training engineers, b) briefing contractors and c) raising community/worker awareness; and

- a well worked out system of monitoring (with pro-forma record sheets, if required).

√ Plan a strategy. As a general principal work outwards, starting with who you know. For example, if you (as the Employer/line ministry) are receiving assistance from several different donors then suggest to these donors that you want to implement labour standards in the programmes they are assisting with.

√ Initially, target programmes located in areas of the country which will use Supervising Engineers and contractors already familiar with labour standards from the pilot.

√ Build labour standards into bid assessment criteria and institutional guidance on procurement.

√ Build a wider constituency for labour standards work by making links with ministries and agencies interested in specific standards. For example, departments of Women's Affairs will be interested in what is being done to prevent discrimination against women on site; the Ministry of Health will be interested in work on HIV/AIDS (and may be helping with this); the department responsible for the national Poverty Reduction Strategy will support the links being made between labour standards, poverty and rural livelihoods.

Box 12. Scaling up in Ghana: proposed strategy from March 2002

A five step strategy for institutionalising labour standards in the construction sector is envisaged.

Step 1. Implement on the DFID assisted *Bridges programme*. This is the pilot which will test all systems for transfer and adaptation elsewhere (1998-2002)

Step 2. Implement on the DFID assisted *Feeder Roads programme* (much bigger and in another part of the country, so will involve a lot more contractor and engineer training). Convenient because DFID is funding so has a definite interest in seeing it succeed (2001-2005)

Step 3. Implement on *all DFR programmes* in Ghana. This means getting other donors who financially support DFR to build in labour standards implementation to their processes - and budgets. This is just beginning with Danida, the EC, GTZ, and the World Bank involved. (2001 onwards)

Step 4. Implement on all *Ministry of Roads and Transport programmes*. This means extending LS to DFR's sister departments, Urban Roads and Highways. This is outside DFR's jurisdiction but within its sphere of influence. Also by this time a good number of the contractors and SEs will have been trained. Both these groups work across the roads sector. (Planned to begin in 2002)

Step 5. Implement throughout Ghana. Starting with all other line departments doing infrastructure work (e.g. Ministry of Works and Housing, Education, Heath etc.) with support from other ministries interested in specific standards (e.g. Women's Affairs, Poverty Reduction).

The Department of Feeder Roads, has 'control' over what happens only with programmes it is responsible for implementing. (Steps 1, 2, 3). However, it can influence decision makers in other ministries (Steps 4 and 5) both directly, and by building up a constituency of others which are supportive of labour standards.

Part 3

Contract clauses and labour standards

Using Part 3 of the Sourcebook

In Part 3 we provide examples of contract clauses which are relevant to labour standards in construction. This follows on directly from the suggestions made in action point 14: *Incorporate labour standards in contract documents (formal contracting) and community contracting agreements*. As stated in action point 14, our objective in doing this is to offer the user some tried and tested examples of clauses for inclusion in construction contracts and further suggestions for making them operational.

Part 3 is divided into three sections

- Section 1   deals with specific contract clauses
- Section 2   provides a starting point for making clauses relating to labour standards operational
- Section 3   considers the specific issue of mainstreaming HIV/AIDS into contractual processes

In Section 1, Box 13 provides the key which relates each of the labour standards to the specific contract clauses we have reviewed; our examples are taken from a number of sources, both international and national. Particular attention is paid to the 4th Edition of FIDIC Conditions of Contract, as these (and its derivatives) are widely used in international procurement. We also provide national examples from India and Ghana. The source of these clauses is identified and a brief description of their content is given.

Box 13 also directs the user to the actual wording of these contract clauses, which is given in full in Boxes 14-18 as follows:

Box   Source details

Box 14 Part 1, 4th Edition of FIDIC Conditions of Contract

Box 15 Part 2, 4th Edition of FIDIC Conditions of Contract

Box 16 Ghana: Feeder Roads Bridges Project, Department of Feeder Roads, Ministry of Roads and Transport, Ghana

Box 17 India: Public Works Department, States of Kerala and Orissa

Box 18 DFID Interim Guidelines 1999

In Section 2, Box 19 provides a checklist which leads in to the next stage, namely the development of specifications to aid the interpretation of the clauses for operational use.

In Section 3, we consider how awareness raising of HIV/AIDS issues can be included in construction contracts, and suggest model forms of contract for inclusion in construction projects.

Section 1: Contract Clauses

In this section, Boxes 13-18 provide details of contract clauses in relation to labour standards in construction

Note: Abbreviation Cl refers to the Clause number as shown in Boxes 14-18

Box 13. Summary of relevant contract clauses

Core Labour Standard	Relevant FIDIC Clauses	Relevant Clauses from other documents
Freedom of Association.		*Ghana Cl 34.10* Contractor must recognise workers right to trade union membership.
Equality of Treatment.		*DFID Cl A* states that men and women should receive equal rates of pay. *DFID Cl K* provides for records to allow monitoring.
Wages 1. **Minimum wages.** 2. **Timeliness of payment.** 3. **Payment records.**	FIDIC Part II Cl 34(i) covers minimum rates of wages.	1. *Ghana Cl 34.2* covers wage rates. *DFID Cl A* states in addition that payment should be in cash. *Ghana Cl 34.5* display notices informing workers of their entitlements, *Cl 34.18* makes it a requirement that the Contractor has paid wage rates of at least the minimum for three months prior to bidding. *India Cl P* makes "fair wage" a requirement. *Cl M* requires the Contractor to pay not less than that paid for similar work in the neighbourhood. 2. *Ghana Cl 34.3* states that employees should be paid promptly and regularly. If the Contractor fails to comply with the above, *Cl 34.19*, *India Cl R* cover payment by the Engineer out of monies due to the Contractor. 3. *Ghana Cl 34.6* covers payment records; *DFID Cl K* is similar but provides for more detailed records to include information on gender and casual/ permanent labour.

Box 13. continued

Core Labour Standard	Relevant FIDIC Clauses	Relevant Clauses from other documents
Working Hours **1. Conditions of work.** **2. Flexibility.**	1. FIDIC Part I Cl 45.1 states that working at night or on recognised days of rest is not allowed. (This is primarily for the convenience of the supervising Engineer). 2. FIDIC Part II Cl 34(xiv) requires the Contractor to have due regard to all recognised festivals, days of rest and religious or other customs.	1. *DFID Cl K* provides for detailed records to include information on hours worked for monitoring purposes. (see also *Ghana Cl 34.6*). *Ghana Cl 34.5* requires the Contractor to display notices informing employees about conditions of work. *India Cl M* requires the Contractor to obtain written permission for work on Sundays and Public Holidays, and to grant a weekly paid holiday to his labourers.
Health and Safety **1. General.**	1. FIDIC Part I Cl 8.2 requires the Contractor to take full responsibility for the safety of all site operations and methods of construction; Cl 19.1 requires him to have full regard for the safety of all persons on the site. FIDIC Part II Cl 34(v) requires the Contractor to employ a qualified Safety Officer; Cl 34(vii) requires the Contractor to protect labour from insect and pest nuisance.	1. *India Cl S* states that the Contractor is responsible for safety of labourers and is liable for compensation payments. *India Cl T* gives the Engineer the right to stop/suspend the work in the interest of safety; the Contractor has no right to compensation for the stoppage. *India Cl M* forbids the employment of female labour within the limits of a cantonment.

Box 13. continued

Core Labour Standard	Relevant FIDIC Clauses	Relevant Clauses from other documents
2. Accident insurance and liability.	2. FIDIC Part I Cl 22.1 & 24.1 states that the Contractor shall indemnify the Employer against losses and claims in respect of death or injury to any person. FIDIC Part I Cl 24.2 requires the Contractor to insure against accidents to workmen, Cl 25.1 requires the Contractor to provide evidence of insurance prior to the start of work and the policies themselves within 84 days, Cl 25.2 states that the insurance should be adequate. Cl 25.3 allows for the Employer to take out insurance if the Contractor fails to do so, and recover the cost from the Contractor.	2. *DFID Cl H* covers the situation where the length of the contract is less than 84 days. *India Cl V* requires the Contractor to insure against claims under the 'Workmen's Compensation Act'.
3. Clothing & equipment.		3. *Ghana Cl 8.3* requires the Contractor to provide workers in hazardous occupations with protective clothing gloves etc.
4. First Aid.	4. FIDIC Part II Cl 34(vi) requires the Contractor to provide first aid equipment.	4. *DFID Cl E* requires the Contractor to supply and maintain appropriate first aid facilities.
5. Procedures.	5. FIDIC Part II Cl 34(viii) requires the Contractor to comply with the requirements of the local authority in the event of an epidemic. FIDIC Part II Cl 35 covers accident records and reports.	5. *Ghana Cl 34.17* details the requirements in the event of an accident on site.

Box 13. continued

Core Labour Standard	Relevant FIDIC Clauses	Relevant Clauses from other documents
6. Amenities: water supply.	6. FIDIC Part II Cl 34(xi) requires the Contractor to provide an adequate supply of drinking water "so far as is reasonably practicable, having regard to local conditions".	6. *Ghana Cl 34.8* strengthens the FIDIC requirement for the Contractor to supply safe drinking water. *India Cl N* requires the Contractor to provide drinking water at his own cost for his labour camp.
7. Amenities: sanitation.	7. FIDIC Part II Cl 34(iv) requires the Contractor to provide sanitation at the accommodation he provides for his labour.	7. *Ghana Cl 34.9* requires the Contractor to provide a specific type of latrine; *DFID Cl D* is similar only does not specify the type of latrine but requires separate arrangements for men and women. *India Cl N* requires the Contractor to provide "sanitary arrangements" at his own cost for his labour camp.
8. Amenities: food.	8. FIDIC Part II Cl 34(x) requires the Contractor to provide suitable food at reasonable prices to his workforce.	8. *DFID Cl F* adds the requirement to provide clean shelters for the consumption of food.
9. Amenities: shelter.	9. FIDIC Part II Cl 34(iv) requires the Contractor to provide, maintain and furnish accommodation for the workers.	9. *Ghana Cl 34.7* requires the Contractor to arrange for the accommodation of his staff and labour.
Casualisation Conditions of work.		*DFID Cl K* provides for detailed records to include information on casual/ permanent labour.
Social Security Regimes Welfare.		*India Cl W* states that 1% of cost of construction to be remitted to the construction workers welfare fund.

Box 13. continued		
Core Labour Standard	**Relevant FIDIC Clauses**	**Relevant Clauses from other documents**
Employment of Children.		*DFID Cl G* forbids the employment of children. *India Cl M* forbids the employment of anyone below the age of 12.
Forced Labour.		(Nothing found)
HIV/Aids.		Separate proposed HIV Clause requires Contractor to provide HIV Awareness Programme (See Section 3).
Other **1. Engagement of labour.**	1. FIDIC Part I Cl 34.1 makes the Contractor responsible for the engagement, payment, housing, feeding and transport of all labour.	1. *Ghana Cl 34.1* encourages the Contractor to employ labour from within Ghana. *India Cl M* requires "tribes of the locality" to be employed as far as possible.
2. Compliance with laws etc.	2. FIDIC Part I Cl 26.1 requires the Contractor to comply with all laws and regulations.	2. *Ghana Cl 34.4* adds that "strict" compliance with labour laws is required.
3. Expatriate labour.	3. FIDIC Part II Cl 34(iii) states that the Contractor is responsible for the repatriation of labour.	3. *Ghana Cl 34.11* states that the Contractor is responsible for the repatriation of any expatriate labour and for conforming with Immigration and Aliens Acts.

Box 14. Clauses from FIDIC Conditions of Contract Part 1

Clause name	No.	Clause
Site Operations and Methods of Construction.	**8.2**	The Contractor shall take full responsibility for the adequacy, stability and safety of all Site operations and methods of construction. Provided that the Contractor shall not be responsible (except as stated hereunder or as may be otherwise agreed) for the design or specification of Permanent Works, or for the design or specification of any Temporary Works not prepared by the Contractor. Where the Contract expressly provides that part of the Permanent Works shall be designed by the Contractor, he shall be fully responsible for that part of such Works, notwithstanding any approval by the Engineer.
Contractor's Employees.	**16.1**	The Contractor shall provide on the Site in connection with the execution and completion of the Works and the remedying of any defects therein: a) only such technical assistants as are skilled and experienced in their respective callings and such foremen and leading hands as are competent to give proper superintendence of the Works, and b) such skilled, semi-skilled and unskilled labour as is necessary for the proper and timely fulfilling of the Contractor's obligations under the Contract.

Clause name	No.	Clause
Safety, Security and Protection of the Environment.	**19.1**	The Contractor shall, throughout the execution and completion of the Works and the remedying of any defects therein:
		a) have full regard for the safety of all persons entitled to be upon the Site and keep the Site (so far as the same is under his control) and the Works (so far as the same are not completed or occupied by the Employer) in an orderly state appropriate to the avoidance of danger to such persons,
		b) provide and maintain at his own cost all lights, guards, fencing, warning signs and watching, when and where necessary or required by the Engineer or by any duly constituted authority, for the protection of the Works or for the safety and convenience of the public or others, and
		c) take all reasonable steps to protect the environment on and off the Site and to avoid damage or nuisance to persons or to property of the public or others resulting from pollution, noise or other causes arising as a consequence of his methods of operation.
Damage to Persons and Property.	**22.1**	The Contractor shall, except if and so far as the Contract provides otherwise, indemnify the Employer against all losses and claims in respect of:
		a) death of or injury to any person, or
		b) loss of or damage to any property (other than the Works),
		which may arise out of or in consequence of the execution and completion of the Works and the remedying of any defects therein, and against all claims, proceedings, damages, costs, charges and expenses whatsoever in respect thereof or in relation thereto, subject to the exceptions defined in Sub-Clause 22.2.

Box 14. continued

69

Box 14. continued

Clause name	No.	Clause
Accident or Injury to Workmen.	**24.1**	The Employer shall not be liable for or in respect of any damages or compensation payable to any workman or other person in the employment of the Contractor or any Subcontractor, other than death or injury resulting from any act or default of the Employer, his agents or servants. The Contractor shall indemnify and keep indemnified the Employer against all such damages and compensation, other than those for which the Employer is liable as aforesaid, and against all claims, proceedings, damages, costs, charges, and expenses whatsoever in respect thereof or in relation thereto.
Insurance Against Accident to Workmen.	**24.2**	The Contractor shall insure against such liability and shall continue such insurance during the whole of the time that any persons are employed by him on the Works. Provided that, in respect of any persons employed by any Subcontractor, the Contractor's obligations to insure as aforesaid under this Sub-Clause shall be satisfied if the Subcontractor shall have insured against the liability in respect of such persons in such manner that the Employer is indemnified under the policy, but the Contractor shall require such Subcontractor to produce to the Employer, when required, such policy of insurance and the receipt for the payment of the current premium.
Evidence and Terms of Insurances.	**25.1**	The Contractor shall provide evidence to the Employer prior to the start of work at the Site that the insurances required under the Contract have been effected and shall, within 84 days of the Commencement Date, provide the insurance policies to the Employer. When providing such evidence and such policies to the Employer, the Contractor shall notify the Engineer of so doing. Such insurance policies shall be consistent with the general terms agreed prior to the issue of the Letter of Acceptance. The Contractor shall effect all insurances for which he is responsible with insurers and in terms approved by the Employer.
Adequacy of Insurances.	**25.2**	The Contractor shall notify the insurers of changes in the nature, extent or programme for the execution of the Works and ensure the adequacy of the insurances at all times in accordance with the terms of the Contract and shall, when required, produce to the Employer the insurance policies in force and the receipts for payment of the current premiums.

Box 14. continued

Clause name	No.	Clause
Remedy on Contractor's Failure to Insure.	**25.3**	If the Contractor fails to effect and keep in force any of the insurances required under the Contract, or fails to provide the policies to the Employer within the period required by Sub-Clause 25.1, then and in any such case the Employer may effect and keep in force any such insurances and pay any premium as may be necessary for that purpose and from time to time deduct the amount so paid from any monies due or to become due to the Contractor, or recover the same as a debt due from the Contractor.
Compliance with Statutes, Regula-tions.	**26.1**	The Contractor shall conform in all respects, including by the giving of all notices and the paying of all fees, with the provisions of: a) any National or State Statute, Ordinance, or other Law, or any regulation, or bye-law of any local or other duly constituted authority in relation to the execution and completion of the Works and the remedying of any defects therein, and b) the rules and regulations of all public bodies and companies whose property or rights are affected or may be affected in any way by the Works, and the Contractor shall keep the Employer indemnified against all penalties and liability of every kind for breach of any such provisions. Provided always that the Employer shall be responsible for obtaining any planning, zoning or other similar permission required for the Works to proceed and shall indemnify the Contractor in accordance with Sub-Clause 22.3.

Box 14. continued

Clause name	No.	Clause
Interference with Traffic and Adjoining Properties.	**29.1**	All operations necessary for the execution and completion of the Works and the remedying of any defects therein shall, so far as compliance with the requirements of the Contract permits, be carried on so as not to interfere unnecessarily or improperly with: a) the convenience of the public, or b) the access to, use and occupation of public or private roads and footpaths to or of properties whether in the possession of the Employer or of any other person. The Contractor shall save harmless and indemnify the Employer in respect of all claims, proceedings, damages, costs, charges and expenses whatsoever arising out of, or in relation to, any such matters insofar as the Contractor is responsible therefor.
Engagement of Staff and Labour.	**34.1**	The Contractor shall, unless otherwise provided in the Contract, make his own arrangements for the engagement of all staff and labour, local or other, and for their payment, housing, feeding and transport.
Returns of Labour and Contractor's Equipment.	**35.1**	The Contractor shall, if required by the Engineer, deliver to the Engineer a return in detail, in such form and at such intervals as the Engineer may prescribe, showing the staff and the numbers of the several classes of labour from time to time employed by the Contractor on the Site and such information respecting Contractor's Equipment as the Engineer may require.
Restriction on Working Hours.	**45.1**	Subject to any provision to the contrary contained in the Contract, none of the Works shall, save as hereinafter provided, be carried on during the night or on locally recognised days of rest without the consent of the Engineer, except when work is unavoidable or absolutely necessary for the saving of life or property or for the safety of the Works, in which case the Contractor shall immediately advise the Engineer. Provided that the provisions of this Clause shall not be applicable in the case of any work which is customary to carry out by multiple shifts.

Box 15. Clauses from FIDIC Conditions of Contract Part 2 - *Example Sub-Clauses*

Clause name	No.	Clause
Language Ability of Contractor's Representative.	15.2	The Contractor's authorised representative shall be fluent in (insert name of language).
Interpreter to be Made Available.	or	If the Contractor's authorised respresentative is not, in the opinion of the Engineer, fluent in (insert name of language), the Contractor shall have available on Site at all times a competent interpreter to ensure the proper transmission of instructions and information.
Language Ability of Superintending Staff.	16.3	A reasonable proportion of the Contractor's superintending staff shall have a working knowledge of (insert name of language) or the Contractor shall have available on Site at all times a sufficient number of competent interpreters to ensure the proper transmission of instructions and information.
Employment of Local Personnel.	16.4	The Contractor is encouraged, to the extent practicable and reasonable, to employ staff and labour from sources within (insert name of country).

Box 15. continued

Clause name	No.	Clause
Rates of Wages and Conditions of Labour.	34 (i)	The Contractor shall pay rates of wages and observe conditions of labour not less favourable than those established for the trade or industry where the work is carried out. In the absence of any rates of wages or conditions of labour so established, the Contractor shall pay rates of wages and observe conditions of labour which are not less favourable than the general level of wages and conditions observed by other employers whose general circumstances in the trade or industry in which the Contractor is engaged are similar.
Employment of Persons in the Service Others.	34 (ii)	The Contractor shall not recruit or attempt to recruit his staff and labour from amongst persons in the service of the Employer or the Engineer.
Repatriation of Labour.	34 (iii)	The Contractor shall be responsible for the return to the place where they were recruited or to their domicile of all such persons as he recruited and employed for the purposes of or in connection with the Contract and shall maintain such persons as are to be so returned in a suitable manner until they shall have left the Site or, in the case of persons who are not nationals of and have been recruited outside (insert name of country), shall have left (insert name of country).
Housing for Labour.	34 (iv)	Save insofar as the Contract otherwise provides, the Contractor shall provide and maintain such accommodation and amenities as he may consider necessary for all his staff and labour, employed for the purposes of or in connection with the Contract, including all fencing, water supply (both for drinking and other purposes), electricity supply, sanitation, cookhouses, fire prevention and fire-fighting equipment, air conditioning, cookers, refrigerators, furniture and other requirements in connection with such accommodation or amenities. On completion of the Contract, unless otherwise agreed with the Employer, the temporary camps/housing provided by the Contractor shall be removed and the site reinstated to its original condition, all to the approval of the Engineer.

Box 15. continued

Clause name	No.	Clause
Accident Prevention Officer; Accidents.	**34** (v)	The Contractor shall have on his staff at the Site an officer dealing only with questions regarding the safety and protection against accidents of all staff and labour. This officer shall be qualified for this work and shall have the authority to issue instructions and shall take protective measures to prevent accidents.
Health and Safety.	**34** (vi)	Due precautions shall be taken by the Contractor, and at his own cost, to ensure the safety of his staff and labour and, in collaboration with and to the requirements of the local health authorities, to ensure that medical staff first aid equipment and stores, sick bay and suitable ambulance service are available at the camps, housing and on the Site at all times throughout the period of the Contract and that suitable arrangements are made for the prevention of epidemics and for all necessary welfare and hygiene require-ments.
Measures against Insect and Pest Nuisance.	**34** (vii)	The Contractor shall at all times take the necessary precautions to protect all staff and labour employed on the site from insect nuisance, rats and other pests and reduce the dangers to health and the general nuisance occasioned by the same. The Contractor shall provide his staff and labour with suitable prophylactics for the prevention of malaria and take steps to prevent the formation of stagnant pools of water. He shall comply with all the regulations of the local health authorities in these respects and shall in particular arrange to spray thoroughly with approved insecticide all buildings erected on the Site. Such treatment shall be carried out at least once a year or as instructed by the Engineer. The Contractor shall warn his staff and labour of the dangers of bilharzia and wild animals.
Epidemics.	**34** (viii)	In the event of any outbreak of illness of an epidemic nature, the Contractor shall comply with and carry out such regulations, orders and requirements as may be made by the Government, or the local medical or sanitary authorities, for the purpose of dealing with and overcoming the same.

Box 15. continued

Clause name	No.	Clause
Burial of the Dead.	34 (ix)	The Contractor shall make all necessary arrangements for the transport, to any place as required for burial, of any of his expatriate employees or members of their families who may die in (insert name of country). The Contractor shall also be responsible, to the extent required by the local regulations, for making any arrangements with regard to burial of any of his local employees who may die while engaged upon the Works.
Supply of Foodstuffs.	34 (x)	The Contractor shall arrange for the provision of a sufficient supply of suitable food at reasonable prices for all his staff, labour and Subcontractors, for the purposes of or in connection with the Contract.
Supply of Water.	34 (xi)	The Contractor shall, so far as is reasonably practicable, having regard to local conditions, provide on the Site an adequate supply of drinking and other water for the use of his staff and labour.
Alcoholic Liquor or Drugs.	34 (xii)	The Contractor shall not, otherwise than in accordance with the Statutes, Ordinances and Government Regulations or Orders for the time being in force, import, sell, give, barter or otherwise dispose of any alcoholic liquor or drugs, or permit or suffer any such importation, sale, gift, barter or disposal by his Subcontractors, agents, staff or labour.
Arms and Ammunition.	34 (xiii)	The Contractor shall not give, barter or otherwise dispose of to any person or persons, any arms or ammunition of any kind or permit or suffer the same as aforesaid.
Festivals and Religious Customs.	34 (xiv)	The Contractor shall in all dealings with his staff and labour have due regard to all recognised festivals, days of rest and religious or other customs.
Disorderly Conduct.	34 (xv)	The Contractor shall at all times take all reasonable precautions to prevent any unlawful, riotous or disorderly conduct by or amongst his staff and labour and for the preservation of peace and protection of persons and property in the neighbourhood of the Works against the same.

Box 15. continued

Clause name	No.	Clause
Records of Safety and Health.	**35**	The Contractor shall maintain such records and make such reports concerning safety, health and welfare of persons and damage to property as the Engineer may from time to time prescribe.
Reporting of Accidents.	**35**	The Contractor shall report to the Engineer details of any accident as soon as possible after its occurrence. In the case of any fatality or serious accident, the Contractor shall, in addition, notify the Engineer immediately by the quickest available means.

Box 16. Ghana Bridges for Feeder Roads Project

Clause reference	Clause name	Clause
8.3	**Protective Clothing.**	The Contractor and any Sub-Contractor engaged in the performance of the contract shall provide and equip, as appropriate, all workers in hazardous occupations with protective clothing, gloves, goggles, masks, footwear and headgear manufactured to such a standard as to ensure adequate protection against injury and accident.
34.1	**Engagement of labour.**	The Contractor shall make his own arrangements for the engagement of all labour, local or otherwise, and save insofar as the contract otherwise provides, for the transport, housing, feeding and payment thereof. The Contractor is encouraged, to the extent practicable and reasonable, to employ staff and labour with the required qualifications and experience from sources within Ghana. The Contractor shall not knowingly employ staff who are in regular employment of the Government, unless the services of such persons are no longer required by the Government.
34.2	**Rates of wages.**	The Contractor shall pay rates of wages not less favourable than those approved by the Government in the District where the Works are being carried out.
34.3	**Payment of wages.**	The Contractor shall pay his employees promptly and regularly at the customary intervals and all employees shall be paid in full and up to date before the issue of the Defects Liability Certificate.
34.4	**Compliance with laws and regulations.**	The Contractor shall comply in all respects with the requirements of all laws for the time being in force and shall ascertain from the Labour Department and shall strictly comply with all the regulations written or otherwise of the Commissioner of Labour or any of his duly appointed representatives affecting the employment of any class of employee under this contract and from time to time in force.
34.5	**Display of provision of this clause.**	The Contractor shall at all times during the continuance of the Contract display in conspicuous places on the site and in the factory or other place occupied by him for the execution of the Contract in positions convenient, reading notices informing his employees of the foregoing provisions of this Clause and of their conditions of work.

Box 16. continued

Clause reference	Clause name	Clause
34.6	**Records of Time Worked and Wages Paid.**	The Contractor shall keep proper records of the time worked by every employee engaged on the Contract, the class of work on which employed and the wages paid. Such records shall be available for inspection at any time by the Engineer or the Engineer's Representative or any duly appointed representative of the Commissioner of Labour, and the Contractor shall produce if required such other records as may be necessary as evidence of his compliance with the requirements of this clause.
34.7	**Contractor's Dwellings.**	The Contractor shall at his own expense make his own arrangements for the accommodation of his staff and labour and shall not make use of Government Rest houses or other Government facilities unless with the express permission of the appropriate authority and on payment of the appropriate charges.
34.8	**Supply of Water.**	The Contractor and Sub-Contractors shall provide on the site, throughout working hours, adequate and easily accessible supplies of safe drinking water and other water for the use of their employees.
34.9	**Temporary Latrines.**	The Contractor shall provide and maintain adequate and sanitary latrine accommodation modelled on the Kumasi Improved Ventilated Pit Latrine and constructed to comply with any Government regulations in force for the use of the employees on the Works and shall keep the whole of the site and latrines in a clean and sanitary condition to the satisfaction of the Engineer and in accordance with the requirements of the Health Authorities of the Government. The Health Officer shall be informed when the Works are about to begin. The Contractor shall thoroughly disinfect and fill all latrine pits, swamps and trenches when no longer required.
34.10	**Trades Union Membership.**	The Contractor or Sub-Contractor shall recognise the freedom of his work people to be members of registered trade unions.

Box 16. continued

Clause reference	Clause name	Clause
34.11	**Expatriate Labour.**	The Contractor shall make his own arrangement for the engagement of expatriate labour and for the housing, health, welfare and repatriation of the same, and shall conform in all respects with the conditions and requirements of the Immigration Act No. 154 of 1957 and the Aliens Act No. 160 of 1963, and any amendments thereto or replacements thereof.
34.17	**Accidents.**	The Contractor shall within 24 hours of the occurrence of any accident at or about the site or in connection with the execution of the Works report such accident to the Engineer's Representative. The Contractor shall also report such accident to the competent authority whenever such report is required by law.
34.18	**Certificate of Compliance.**	The Contractor shall, in respect of all persons employed by him (whether in the execution of the Contract or otherwise), in every factory workshop or place used by him for the execution of the Contract comply with sub-clause 34.4 and, if required by the Government, shall before entering into the Contract certify that to the best of his knowledge and belief he has complied with sub-clause 34.2 for three months immediately preceding the date of submission of the Bid.
34.19	**Default of Payment of Wages.**	In the event of default being made in payment of wages of any workmen employed on the Contract, and, if a claim thereafter is filed in the office of the Engineer's Representative and satisfactory proof thereof furnished, the Engineer shall be notified forthwith and may, failing payment by the Contractor, arrange the payment of such claim out of the monies at any time payable under the Contract and the amount so paid shall be deemed payments to the Contractor under the Contract.

Box 17. India: Public Works Departments (Orissa and Kerala)

Clause reference	Clause name	Clause
M	Engagement of Labour.	
	(Women)	No Female labourer shall be employed within the limits of a cantonment.
	(Child Labour)	The contractor shall not employ, for the purpose of this contract, any person, who is below the age of twelve years and shall pay to each labourer, for the work done by such labourer wages not less than the wages paid for similar work in the neighbourhood.The Engineer-in-charge and/or Assistant Engineer and/or Engineer-subordinate in immediate charge of the work shall have the right to decide whether any labourer employed by the contractor is below the age of twelve years and to refuse to allow any labourer, when he decides him/her to be below the age of twelve years, to be employed by the contractor.
	(Wages)	The Engineer-in-charge shall have the right to enquire into and decide any complaint alleging that the wages, paid by the contractor to any labourer, for the work done by such labourer, is less than the wage paid for similar work in the neighbourhood.
	(Working hours)	The contractor shall have to grant a weekly paid holiday to his labourers/staff. For carrying out the work on Sundays and public Holidays on exceptional circumstance, the contractor shall have to obtain prior written permission from the Authority. The contractor shall have to comply all other labour legislations.
	(Local labour)	Tribes of the locality should be employed to the extent possible.

Box 17. continued

Clause reference	Clause name	Clause
N	**Sanitary arrangements.**	Sanitary arrangements and supply of drinking water will be made by the contractor at his own cost for his labour camp.
P	**Fair wages.**	The contractor should pay fair wages to the labour engaged on the work which will be fixed by the Government as specified in Government Order (18-8597j/55/LD) dated (7th March 1956) and any dues to the labour will be recovered from his bill as fixed by the departmental officers.
R	**Payment.**	The Executive Engineer or Subdivision Officer concerned shall have the right to deduct from the moneys due to the contractor any required or intimated to be required for making good the loss suffered by a worker by reason of non-fulfilment of the conditions of contract for the benefit of workers, non-payment of wages or deductions made from his or their wages which are not justified by their terms of the contract or non observance of regulations.
S	**Safety.**	The contractor shall be responsible for the safety of the labour employed by him and he shall be liable to pay the necessary compensation in case of accidents, as per the Workman's Compensation Act.
T	**Safety.**	The Engineer-in-charge shall have the right to stop/suspend the work temporarily, for any reason, adversely affecting the interest/safety of the work. The contractor shall have no objection to such stoppage of work and shall have no right for claiming compensation for such stoppage.

Box 17. continued

Clause reference	Clause name	Clause
V	**Idemnity.**	It shall be the contractors sole responsibility to protect the public and his employees against accident from any cause and he shall indemnify Government against any claims for damages for injury to person or property, resulting from any such accidents and he shall where the provisions of the workman's Compensation Act apply, take steps to properly insure against any claim there under.
W	**Social security regimes.**	As part of Section 8(3) of the Kerala Construction Workers Welfare Fund act 1989 it is the responsibility of the departments, Corporations or Boards as the case may be to deduct the employers contribution (1%) from the bills of the contractors and to remit the amount in the account of Kerala Construction Workers Welfare Fund within 15 days from the date of such deductions. While working out the total cost the value of the departmental materials supplied will be included.

Box 18. DFID Interim Guidelines: proposed Clauses

Clause reference	Clause name	Clause Note: these clauses are untested
A	Rates of Wages.	The Contractor shall pay rates of wages not less favourable than those approved by the government for the various classes of labour engaged. All payments shall be in cash unless employees request, in writing, payment by cheque or other negotiable financial instrument. Payment in kind or through trade goods of any sort is prohibited. Food rations, accommodation, or any other allowances will be over and above cash wages complying with the minimum levels described. Men and women shall receive equal rates of pay for the particular grade of work, trade or skill for which they are employed.
B	Payment of Wages.	The Contractor shall pay his/her employees promptly and regularly at the customary intervals, or as may be prescribed by law, and all employees shall be paid in full and up to date before the issue of the Engineer's Maintenance Certificate .
C	Default of Payment of Wages.	In the event of default in payment of wages to any worker employed on the contract, by the Contractor or his/her Subcontractor(s), and, if a claim with satisfactory proof thereof is received by the Engineer, the Engineer may make the payment of such a claim out of the monies at any time payable under the contract, and the amount so paid shall be deemed payments to the contractor or sub-contractors under the contract.
D	Temporary Latrines.	The Contractor shall provide and maintain efficient, adequate and sanitary latrine and washing facilities constructed to comply with any government regulation in force for the use of the employees on the works, with separate arrangements for men and women, and shall keep the whole of the site and latrines in a clean and sanitary condition to the satisfaction of the Engineer, and in accordance with the requirements of the health authorities of the government. The Contractor shall thoroughly disinfect and fill all latrine pits, swamps and trenches when no longer required.

Box 18. continued

Clause reference	Clause name	Clause Note: these clauses are untested
E	**First Aid.**	The Contractor shall provide and maintain adequate first aid facilities appropriate to the conditions and scope of the works, and shall submit for the engineer's approval details of those facilities and the means by which full access to them and their administration will be provided. Scale of first aid facilities will be related to the size of the job. There also needs to be provision for arrangements to evacuate injured persons to a health centre, for which the responsibility lies with the engineer and contractor
F	**Food.**	The contractor shall ensure the provision of adequate and suitable nutritious food at affordable cost to all workers engaged on the works, and provide suitable clean shelters(s) appropriately furnished for the consumption of food.
G	**Employment of children.**	Children as defined by government regulation shall not be employed under any circumstances.
H	**Insurance.**	notwithstanding the provisions of clause 25.1, part I, the contractor shall provide to the employer, prior to the start of the work at the site, the insurance policies required under the contract. When providing such policies to the employer, the contractor shall notify the engineer of so doing.
K	**Records.**	The contractor shall keep proper records of the days, dates and hours worked by every employee engaged on the contract, their gender, the class of work in which employed, whether as a casual or permanent employee, and the wages (and allowances if any), paid. These records shall be available at any time for inspection by the Engineer or the Engineer's representative or any authorised representative of the government. Monthly summaries in a format to be agreed by the Engineer will be forwarded to the Employer.

Section 2: Making clauses operational

Contract clauses may often express an intention to do something. How it will be done is often not specified and this can lead to problems when the clauses are implemented if either (or both) the employer and contractor lack experience in dealing with labour standards. In most cases, the *intentions* which are expressed in contract clauses are made operational through the use of detailed specifications which provide an additional level of detail. This additional detail enables the contractor to implement the requirements of the contract clauses and assists the employer in monitoring and approving progress.

Box 19 takes each labour standard and provides a checklist of detailed points to help to get started with developing the specification in relation to labour standards. Many of the points in the checklist raise yet further issues which require decisions to be made. For example, under health and safety, what protective clothing should be provided? It is difficult to be more prescriptive in providing details about this and other points, as these will depend upon location and the nature of the work to be carried out.

Throughout this Sourcebook we have emphasised the importance of the process for introducing labour standards. The overall outcome of improved labour standards also depends on resolving many highly detailed technical and procedural points; the checklist in Box 19 gives some indication of the extent of this.

Box 19. Getting Started	
Labour Standards	**Checklist for "getting started"**
Health and Safety to be assured.	**Clothing & equipment:** ■ What is to be provided ■ Responsibility for procurement and payment ■ Responsibility for storage and issue **First Aid:** ■ Contents of equipment/kits to be provided ■ Number and location of equipment/kits ■ Checking, replenishing and updating contents ■ Designated persons trained in first aid ■ Notifying local clinics or health centres about the works

Box 19. continued	
Labour Standards	**Checklist for "getting started"**
	Procedures: ■ If treatment is required, who treats and who pays? ■ Appointment of a safety officer. ■ Maintaining records of accidents. **Amenities: water supply**: ■ Level of service e.g. per capita quantities, location of supply. points, source of water, measures to protect water quality. ■ Washing and bathing facilities/designated areas. **Amenities: sanitation** ■ Number of latrine cubicles, separate male/female facilities. ■ Design for latrine superstructure and disposal system (e.g. pit, septic tank). **Amenities: food** ■ Provision of canteen if appropriate. **Amenities: shelter** ■ Provision of shelter for non-local workers if appropriate.
Social Security regimes to be applied.	**Welfare:** ■ Registration of workers with the social security agency. ■ Employers contributions to any scheme. ■ Employees contributions to any scheme. ■ Maintaining records of employees registration. **Accident insurance cover:** ■ Employers protection against serious accidents involving death and physical disability for employees. ■ Registration with state or national insurance cover schemes. ■ Details of cover provided e.g. for both permanent and casual workers. ■ Maintaining records of insurance cover.
Wages to be sufficient, to comply with minima, to be paid promptly.	**Minimum wages:** ■ Complying with legal minimum wages locally and/or nationally. **Pay records:** ■ Maintaining records of payment to employees (normal and overtime). ■ Rates of pay for normal time and overtime. ■ Dates/times at which wages paid.

Box 19. continued

Labour Standards	Checklist for "getting started"
Working hours to be regulated.	**Conditions of Work:** ■ Number of normal working hours per day or per week. ■ Timing of normal working hours. ■ Overtime working, whether voluntary or obligatory. ■ Requirements to work "unsocial times" or shifts. **Flexibility:** ■ Altering working hours to suit working mothers. ■ Working hours taking account of seasonal responsibilities.
No deliberate casualisation , equality of treatment for casuals.	**Conditions of Work:** ■ Definitions of "permanent" or "casual" workers. ■ Restrictions or otherwise on the use of casual workers. ■ Differences in pay and/or conditions for casuals/permanent.
Equality of treatment.	**Gender disparity:** ■ Disparity in wages between men and women. ■ Quotas/guidelines for numbers of men/women employed. ■ Use of pay records as a means of monitoring.
Freedom of Association.	**Trade Unions:** ■ Recruitment and organisation of labour. ■ Restrictions on workers registering with trade unions. ■ Role of trade union as intermediaries.
No forced labour. Employment of children to be restricted.	**Child labour:** ■ Prohibition on employment. ■ Restrictions on employment by age or activity.

Section 3: HIV AIDS

Background

Although not itself a labour standard, there is widespread global concern regarding the impact of HIV/AIDS. The execution of an infrastructure contract can involve hiring a large labour force that can be indigenous to the area as well as coming from elsewhere. Mobile populations, including casual, semiskilled and skilled workers, are often part of this work force. Such mobile populations are particularly vulnerable to, and contribute towards the spread of HIV/AIDS. The primary interest of employers and their contractors is to complete contracts on time, within the estimated cost and to the specified quality, and accordingly often prefer to import its experienced labour force rather than use local labour. Inevitably, local community members will interact with workers from outside the project area but neither group is likely to be fully aware of HIV/AIDS or how it can affect their lives. Existing contracts do not provide any incentive for a contractor to provide an HIV/AIDS awareness raising and prevention programme, even if the employer, who is often the government, sees this as desirable and necessary. Thus, in this section we look at the use of contractual mechanisms to facilitate HIV awareness raising and prevention campaigns on infrastructure construction projects.

Contractual Mechanisms

Discussion of the actual implementation of HIV/AIDS awareness raising and prevention programmes is outside the scope of this sourcebook; our concern is how to ensure that such programmes are made an integral part of projects involving the construction of infrastructure. In general, there are two approaches.

Option 1: the contractor is responsible for delivery of the HIV/AIDS awareness raising and prevention programme through a contractual requirement to sub-contract a specialist service provider for the programme. The following documentation has been developed by DFID and is proposed for use in construction contracts:

- Box 20: Notification that the employer would like the contractor to facilitate an HIV/AIDS awareness raising and prevention campaign;

- Box 21: A draft contract clause setting out the details of how this will be done; and

- Box 22: A model agreement between the contractor and an approved service provider for delivery of the HIV campaign.

Option 2: the employer/client is responsible for delivery of the HIV/AIDS awareness raising and prevention programme for the contractors staff through a separate contract with a specialist service provider. This requires the construction contract to contain a short clause stating that HIV/AIDS awareness raising and prevention work will be carried out by the service provider as approved by the employer. The clause places an obligation on the contractor to ensure that workers are able and permitted to attend the programme and that a suitable venue on the site is provided. The model agreement in Box 22 could be slightly modified to form the basis of a contract between the service provider and the employer.

Each option has specific advantages and disadvantages. The capacity of local contractors, employers/clients and their engineers is likely to be a key considerations in deciding which option is best suited to a particular situation. The additional responsibilities include procuring the service and monitoring the delivery of the programme (by the specialist provider) to ensure it is done in accordance with the required specification. Action point 17 refers to issues and problems in monitoring compliance.

Assigning prime responsibility to the contractor provides an apparently straightforward mechanism. The HIV/AIDS prevention service providers are specialists, like any number of other service providers, and are viewed as part of the Contract procurement process. However, lack of capacity in the key functions of construction contracting (delivering on time, cost and quality) is a major problem with small and medium contractors in a number of countries. Additional organisational and supervisory responsibilities around the HIV/AIDS programmes may detract further from the delivery of satisfactory construction of infrastructure and result in poor performance of the HIV/AIDS programme. This is likely to be an important factor in determining which option to adopt.

Box 20. Explanatory Note for inclusion in Invitation to Tender documents

Clause [   ] requires the Contractor to arrange for its employees, its sub-contractor's employees and others to attend an HIV awareness programme provided in accordance with [the project documentation/UNAIDS guidelines] by an organisation approved by the relevant National HIV/AIDS Authority, [*name*].

The programme will be provided at the Employer's cost, though the Contractor will make the initial payment to the programme provider before claiming reimbursement from the Employer in the usual way. The programme will take place during its employees' normal working hours. In pricing his bid, the Contractor should therefore take into account the 'down time' during which employees attend the programme.

This element of the Project will be subject to the normal Project monitoring process.

Further information about the HIV awareness programme (e.g. approved providers of the programme, its cost, duration and content) [is contained in the Project Documentation/ available from UNAIDS at **[contact details]**.

Box 21.   HIV Clause for inclusion in construction contracts

1.1.   For the purpose of this Clause:

"an Approved Service Provider" means a person or entity approved by the National HIV/AIDS Authority to provide the HIV Awareness Programme;

"the Contractor's Employees" means, without prejudice to any other definition contained in the Contract, all workers who are under the Contractor's control and on the Site in connection with the Contract, including any workers who are under the control of any person or entity to whom the Contractor has sub-contracted any of its obligations under the Contract other than those responsibilities set out in this Clause;

"the HIV Awareness Programme" means an HIV awareness programme [as set out in the Project documentation/in compliance with the HIV Awareness Programme curriculum and guidelines published by UNAIDS and available on its website www.hiv-development.org or on request];

"the Local Community" means the communities local to the Site most likely to have contact with the Contractor's Employees and, in particular, sex workers in those communities;

"National Aids Authority" shall mean the authority in the country where the Site is located designated by the relevant national government to have responsibility for preventing and/or combating HIV/AIDS;

"UNAIDS" shall mean [the agency of the United Nations of that name or the United Nations Regional Task Force on mobile population and HIV vulnerability].

1.2.   It shall be a Condition of the Contract that the Contractor:

1.2.1   sub-contracts with an Approved Service Provider to provide an HIV Awareness Programme to the Contractor's Employees and the Local Community as soon as practicable after the Contractor's Employees arrive at the Site but in any case within two weeks after the Contractor's Employees arrive at Site;

1.2.2   gives any representative of the Approved Service Provider, the Employer and the National HIV/AIDS Authority all reasonable access to the Site in connection with the HIV Awareness Programme;

1.2.3   if the National Aids Authority has not provided the names of available Approved Service Providers within two weeks after being asked the contractor may select its own service provider after consultations with the appropriate UNAIDS office;

1.2.4   instructs the Contractor's Employees to attend the HIV Awareness Programme in the course of their employment and during their normal working hours or any period of overtime provided for in the relevant employment contracts and uses all reasonable endeavours to ensure this instruction is followed;

Box 21.   continued

1.2.5   provides suitable space for delivery of the HIV Awareness Programme and does nothing to dissuade the Contractor's Employees from attending the HIV Awareness Programme;

1.2.6   as soon as practicable, notifies the National HIV/AIDS Authority of its sub-contract with an Approved Service Provider to facilitate the National HIV/AIDS Authority's audit of Approved Service Providers; and

1.2.7   gives all reasonable co-operation to the National HIV/AIDS Authority if it exercises its right to audit the provision by the Approved Service Provider of the HIV Awareness Programme.

1.3.   The Contractor shall be entitled to be reimbursed by the Employer for any payments made under a sub-contract made for the purpose of Clause [1.2.1] in accordance with the relevant provisions in the Contract.

1.4.   Where the Contract does not provide for reimbursement of named costs, the amount paid by the Contractor to the Approved Service Provider shall be added to any lump sum to be paid by the Employer to the Contractor under the Contract and, before such lump sum is paid, the Contractor shall provide to the Employer evidence of:

1.4.1   payment of the amount claimed to the Approved Service Provider; and

1.4.2   provision of the HIV Awareness Programme (e.g. a certificate issued by the Approved Service Provider).

1.5.   Where a clinic is provided on behalf of the Contractor on Site, the Contractor shall ensure that such clinic provides to the Contractor's Employees, on request and without charge:

1.5.1   counselling and advice on AIDS in compliance with UNAIDS guidelines; and

1.5.2   condoms that comply with either the current ISO standard or WHO/UNAIDS Specification and Guidelines for Condoms 1998 or any more recent equivalent publication to a maximum of [*number*] per member of the Contractor's Employees per year on a [weekly/monthly] basis.

1.6 .   Where the Contractor sub-contracts any of its obligations under the Contract, it shall require any sub-contractor to comply with sub-clauses [1.2.2 to 1.2.6] of the Contract as if it were the Contractor.

Box 22.   Contract for the provision of an HIV awareness programme to the contractor's employees and others

[UNAIDS/other distributing organisation] has provided this model contract free of charge to the executing parties. It is the responsibility of the parties to ensure the model contract is appropriate to their needs and to amend the model contract as they see fit and to seek independent legal advice as necessary. [UNAIDS/other distributing organisation] accepts no liability for any loss howsoever arising in relation to the use of this model contract.

THIS CONTRACT is made on the [   ] day of [   ] 20[   ]

BETWEEN:
(1)   [................................] ("the Contractor"); and

(2)   [................................] ("the Approved Service Provider").

WHEREAS:
A. the Contractor has established or intends to establish a construction site in [*location*] ("the Site") in connection with a contract between the [*Employer/Client*] and the Contractor ("the Construction Contract");
B. the establishment of construction sites is associated with the increased risk of the transfer of the HIV virus between and among construction workers and the local community;
C. the Contractor has undertaken in the Construction Contract to take certain measures to raise awareness amongst the construction workers at the Site and the local community of the risk of infection with the HIV virus; and
D. the Approved Service Provider has agreed to provide certain HIV awareness-raising activities and services.

IT IS HEREBY AGREED as follows:
1. In this Contract:

"Approved Service Provider" means the organisation named above, provided it has been approved by the National HIV/AIDS Authority for the country in which the Site is located;

"Contractor's Employees" means all workers under the control of the Contractor or any of its sub-contractors (other than the Approved Service Provider) who are at times on the Site in connection with the Construction Contract;

"HIV Awareness Programme" means an HIV awareness programme as provided in the project documentation or in accordance with UNAIDS guidelines available on its website www.hiv-development.org or on request;

"Local Community" means the communities local to the Site which are most likely to have contact with the Contractor's Employees and, in particular, sex workers in those communities;

Box 22. continued

"National HIV/AIDS Authority" means the authority in the country where the Site is located designated by the relevant national government to have responsibility for preventing and/or combating HIV/AIDS; and

"UNAIDS"means the agency of the United Nations of that name.

2. The Approved Service Provider will begin providing the HIV Awareness Programme in accordance with the project documentation or UNAIDS guidelines to the Contractor's Employees and the Local Community as soon as possible after signing this Contract but, in any case, within 2 weeks after the Contractor's Employees arrive at the Site.

3. The Contractor will give the Approved Service Provider all reasonable access to the Site for the purpose of providing the HIV Awareness Programme.

4. The Contractor must make sure the Contractor's Employees are available to attend the HIV Awareness Programme at the times reasonably arranged by the Approved Service Provider (in consultation with the Contractor).

5. The Contractor must do nothing to dissuade the Contractor's Employees from attending the HIV Awareness Programme.

6. In exchange for the provision of the HIV Awareness Programme, the Contractor will pay the Approved Service Provider (exclusive of VAT or any equivalent tax) [*fixed fee*] [*currency*] for the initial phase and [*fixed fee*] [*currency*] for each follow-up phase of the HIV Awareness Programme.

7. When the Approved Service Provider completes the provision of a phase of the HIV Awareness Programme, it will promptly give the Contractor an invoice. The Contractor will pay the Approved Service Provider the amount invoiced no later than 30 days after receiving the invoice.

8. This Contract and all matters arising from or connected with it shall be governed by the law of and subject to the jurisdiction of the courts of the country in which the Site is located [or, if more than one Site, the Site where the Approved Service Provider predominantly provided the HIV Awareness Programme].

IN WITNESS WHEREOF the Contractor and the Approved Service Provider have entered into this Contract as of the day and year first above written:

For and on behalf of   )
[Name of Contractor]   )
                          _____
                          Duly Authorised

For and on behalf of   )
[Name of Approved   )
Service Provider]   )   _____
                          Duly Authorised

Appendix 1

Sample Terms of Reference for a baseline study to address labour standards in community contracting construction work

Introduction

These Terms of Reference have been prepared based on experience gained while undertaking the Social Aspects of Construction Study funded by DFID. Their adaptation will be required depending on the local context, and in consultation with the project stakeholders. It is envisaged that local consultants will be used.

Purpose

The purpose of such a consultancy is to develop baseline information regarding social aspects of construction contracts to inform the development of appropriate measures to protect the rights of workers.

Output

The output from this stage will be a report outlining the results of the baseline survey for each of the construction case studies. The report will also include draft options for assisting the client in applying labour standards in community contracting contexts. The options will be agreed with the client

Activity 1: Review of legal and regulatory framework

For each of the nine labour standards review relevant national/state legislation which may include:

- labour laws in relation to construction workers, working hours, payment of wages, minimum wages, inter-state migration legislation (if relevant)

- social security such as workmen's compensation, welfare acts

- health/accident insurance schemes, and whether there is provision for informal sector/casual workers to participate

- child labour legislation

- equality legislation such as equity in remuneration, equal opportunities (gender, disability, migrants)

- trade union/freedom of association legislation

- the application of such legislation in the community contract

- its application in practice, on site

Activity 2: Case Studies

Short case studies of a cross section of infrastructure projects:

Topic 1: Health and Safety, *to include for example:*

Protective measures :

- what measures are taken to reduce the likelihood of accidents during construction?

- use of protective garments used (boots, gloves, hats etc) and who provided them? how are they procured, maintained and stored? system for monitoring usage?

- are there any simple precautions which stakeholders think could be taken and that they would be willing to promote in order to reduce the risk of accidents i.e. what are their priorities?

Accidents:

- what is the nature and extent of accidents amongst men/women/children?

- details of any minor or major accidents which have led to the concerned person being prevented from working as a result of the accident

- whether any first aid facilities available on the site, for example a simple first aid box, and the system for storage, replenishment, usage. What other medical treatment is available?

- interviewees perceptions about whom they think would be responsible in the event of an accident

- who would treat the injury and who would pay for the treatment?

- any difference between the treatment of skilled and unskilled workers, or between permanent or casual workers?

Facilities:
- are any facilities such as canteen, clean drinking water and latrines provided; any arrangements for providing these informally e.g. from local houses?

- from women's perspective what are the priority facilities to be provided in large and in small projects?

Topic 2: Wages, *to include for example:*
- are minimum wages being adhered to for both men and women, migrants/local workers?

- are wages paid commensurate with other comparable wage rates e.g. in formal contracting or agricultural work?

- how long do labourers have to wait to receive their wages for the work they do? In the opinion of the labourers, is this soon enough and if not what do they perceive to be the reasons for the delay?

- do men and women, migrants and local workers receive equal rates of pay? If not, what is the disparity and why do the informants believe this to happen?

- are any of the workers unionised?

- do the trade unions play any role in community contracting projects?

- suggestions for change

Topic 3: Working Hours, *to include for example:*
- what are the typical number of hours worked by skilled and unskilled, men and women labourers in any one day?

- are workers obliged to work overtime, and is this paid?

- are women required to work after 7 p.m. in the evenings?

- are there many occasions when this exceeds eight hours?

- if much of the work force is casual, is account taken of their other seasonal demands?

Topic 4: Equality of treatment:

- what is the division of labour between men and women on construction sites? Do women have equal access to paid work? How is labour recruited and organized – e.g. do they rely on male channels of communications, or traditional construction work channels?

- what proportion of unskilled workers are women?

- are any training opportunities provided to women? If not, can opportunities for skills training be included in the project?

- do women consider that they are treated equally with male workers?

- do women endure physical and verbal abuse on sites?

- are women sexually exploited on sites?

- how do women balance their other responsibilities; do they bring children to the worksite; is there any risk to the health of women or their children?

- do casual workers consider that they are treated fairly compared with permanent workers?

Topic 5: Social Security, to include for example

- are many of the labourers covered by the Workmen's Compensation Act; if not, is there accident insurance?

- are both permanent and casual workers registered with the national/state social security system? If yes, are payments made from the project to the social security system? If no, are workers interested in being registered and what would be the benefits, if any?

- have there been any claims during the project? What is the nature of the claim? Is there any difference in terms of the nature and frequency of claim by men and women?

- what are labourers priorities in terms of social security?

Topic 6: Child Labour, to include for example:

- does child labour exist either on the site – this could be paid or unpaid while assisting parents?

- are women accompanied by their children? If so, what proportion of women bring their children (local, migrants). What facilities should be provided for children?

- what particular risks are faced by children?

- does child labour exist in the chain of works e.g. in crushing aggregate?

- if it does not exist among local workers, does it exist among migrant workers?

- if found, try to get an understanding of why is it happening and workers suggestions on how it can be reduced and ultimately eliminated

Topic 7: Freedom of association
- are there any local trade unions that are involved with/interested in workers rights in community contracting? If yes, what role do they play?

- are there any community groups that represent workers rights and are these recognised by the client?

- do trade unions or other associations represent women's interests, or the interests of minority workers?

- document any examples of such actions

Topic 8: No forced labour
Because the work is being carried out under the auspices of the community, are workers obliged, implicitly or explicitly, to work? If yes, what are their views on the appropriateness of such a requirement?

Topic 9: No deliberate casualisation
The nature of community contracting suggests that a majority of workers are casual workers. However, check in case there are some skilled workers who should have the benefits of permanent employment e.g. if they form a core skilled group that move from site to site.

- are women likely to be made redundant more than male workers?

- do women fear for their jobs if they assert their rights?

Topic 10: Institutional Issues
- who is responsible for overseeing implementation; how are they selected/ elected?

- what are the mechanisms used to recruit skilled and unskilled labour paid labour?

- who is responsible for monitoring the work? For example: quality of construction (how often and what criteria does it use); the transfer of money from one party to another including scrutiny of bills; recruitment and payment of labour; inspection and audit of files; the award of contracts to particular parties.

- in the opinion of the different respondents, how effective is the monitoring system in ensuring 'fair play'. If there are problems, how could these be overcome?

Activity 3: Implementation, analysis and writing up

The study should be piloted to ensure that the team carrying out the survey are fully appraised of the issues. A review of this will suggest refinements to the methodology and recommend a reporting format for the remaining case studies.

Team members will maintain a field diary, from which the analysis and reports will be prepared in the format that addressed each of the topic areas above; this will be modified accordingly after the pilot stage.

A rapid preliminary analysis will be undertaken and shared with the commissioning organisation.

Following this discussion on the findings, the team will finalise the report for each case study, if relevant.

Following submission of all of the case study reports and raw data, the team in conjunction with the client, will draw up a list of draft options to be considered for implementation in forthcoming construction activities.

Workplan and Approach

The case study work under Activity 1 will be carried out by a team of two persons from the Local Consultants; ideally this should involve both social development and engineering disciplines, at least one of whom shall be female.

All proposed activities must be discussed and agreed with the project partner in this work.

Appropriate techniques and tools are to be determined by the Local Consultants team and are likely to include field visits, site inspections, focus group discussions and key informant interviews and file analysis.

An important source of information is the project files maintained by the concerned Engineer/foreman/other responsible person. The Local Consultants should request to inspect the relevant files, and make full notes of the procedures which have been followed, and examine the muster roll.

Appendix 2

Examples of Specification Clauses used in Bridges for Feeder Roads project, Ghana

Protective clothing

List of protective clothing per employee (includes supervisors):

Steel toe-capped safety boots
Overalls
Safety helmet
Gloves

Additional clothing / equipment for specific tasks:

Raincoat for wet work
Wellington boots for wet work
Dust masks for concrete work
Safety goggles for concrete work
Ear defenders/plugs for noisy work

First Aid kit

Contents of standard kit to include:

Ordinary Bandages	Surgical Blade	Linament
Elastic Bandages	Scissors	Chloroquine
Triangular Bandage	Measuring Cup	Brufen
Cotton Wool	Eye Rinsing Cup	Tricilicate
Plasters	Washing Bowl	Parazone
Lint	Toilet Soap	Oral Re-hydration Salts
Gauze	Gentian Violet Paint	Antacid
Surgical Gloves	Eyewash	Paracetamol
Safety Pins	Disinfectant	
Tweezers	Iodine	

The first aid box is to list the items contained and display expiry dates.
The Contractor is to replace items when exhausted or become out of date.

Safety Committee

The Contractor shall establish a safety committee during the site mobilisation period which is to comprise:

- Contractor's Safety Officer

- Engineer's Representative

- One workers representative from each site

The committee is to meet monthly and present a report / minutes to the monthly progress meeting.

Emergency procedures

The Contractor shall establish emergency evacuation procedures to enable rapid response to accidents, viz. establish contact with local clinics and district hospitals, make arrangements for transport etc.

Record Keeping

The Contractor shall maintain records of employment for all employees engaged on site work. Standard format sheets are to be adopted, as indicated below, which comprise: employment records, work records, pay records and accident records.

Records are to be kept contemporaneously by the Contractor and presented for inspection at monthly meetings. Records are to be kept at site for inspection at any time by the Engineer's Representative.

Records are to be maintained from Day 1 of the contract.

Employee particulars

The Contractor shall record the particulars of each employee as follows:

- Employee name

- Age

- Marital status

- Sex

- Social security number

- Home town

- Address / house number
- Previous employment
- Date of employment
- Date of termination
- Membership of union

Work Records

The Contractor shall record the working hours of each employee for each working day using the sample table as follows:

Contract No: ……………………..
Name of Contractor: …………………………..
Date: ………………………….

Name	Sex	Casual or Permanent	Absent / Present	Reason for Absence	Start Time	Close Time	Overtime Hours	Work Done	Remarks

Pay Records

The Contractor shall record the pay of each employee using the sample table as follows:

Contract No: ………………………..
Name of Contractor: ………………………….
Month/year: ………………………………………

Name	Sex	Status	Basic Pay	Overtime Pay	Gross Pay	Social Security	Tax	TUC Dues	Net Pay	Signature

Accident Records

The Contractor shall record all accidents on the site using the sample table as follows:

Contract No: ……………………………..
Name of Contractor: ……………………….

Month	Accident No	Date / Time	Name	Accident Type	Injuries Sustained	Damage to Property etc	Measures Taken	Remarks
Jan	1							
	2							
	etc							
Feb	1							
	2							
	etc							

Additional bill of quantities items

These items relate to the inclusion of labour standards in the construction contract

ITEM	DESCRIPTION	QTY	UNIT	RATE	AMOUNT
	BILL NO. 1 - GENERAL ITEMS & CONTRACTUAL REQUIREMENTS				
1.	Allow for access to Approved Service Provider for delivery of the HIV Awareness Programme (provisional)		day		
2.	Provide and maintain protective clothing, safety equipment and first aid box for the use of the site employees		sum		
3.	Replacement of protective clothing, equipment and first aid kit items (provisional)		p sum		
4.	Provide water storage tanks (1 No per site)		sum		
5.	Provide safe drinking water for the site employees		sum		
6.	Provide and maintain sanitary latrine accommodation and remove on completion		sum		
7.	Provision of washing area for local inhabitants (provisional)		p sum		
8.	Keeping of employment records		sum		
9.	Preparation of Environmental Management Plan (EMP)		sum		
10.	Meeting all obligations imposed by CC Cl. 19 and those of the EMP		sum		
11.	Percentage adjustment on items 1, 2,.3, 4, 5 and.7 for exceptional compliance with Labour Standards clauses (provisional)		%		

www.ingramcontent.com/pod-product-compliance
Lightning Source LLC
Chambersburg PA
CBHW051611030426

42334CB00035B/3492